AMERICA ENTANGLED

The Persian Gulf Crisis and Its Consequences

D1528214

AMERICA ENTANGLED

The Persian Gulf Crisis and Its Consequences

edited by
Ted Galen Carpenter

CATO
INSTITUTE
Washington D.C.

Library of Congress Cataloging-in-Publication Data

America entangled : the Persian Gulf crisis and its consequences / edited
by Ted Galen Carpenter
    p. cm.
    Includes bibliographical references.
    ISBN 0-932790-85-2 : $8.95.
    1. Persian Gulf War, 1991.   2. United States—Relations—Middle
East   3. Middle East—Relations—United States.   4. United
States—Foreign Relations—1989— I. Carpenter, Ted Galen
DS79.72.A47   1991   91-16424
327.73056—dc20   CIP

Printed in the United States of America.

CATO INSTITUTE
224 Second Street, S.E.
Washington, D.C. 20003

Contents

Introduction

The U.S.-led coalition's decisive victory over Iraq has led to virtual euphoria in some circles. Various officials and pundits are insisting that the outcome of the war demonstrates that the United States is the sole remaining superpower and can police the international system to prevent other outbreaks of aggression. (That position is exemplified by syndicated columnist Charles Krauthammer's "unipolar" thesis.) The "Vietnam syndrome" is dead, they proclaim, and opponents of President Bush's Persian Gulf intervention have been discredited. Indeed, portions of the foreign policy community are experiencing an intoxication of power the like of which has not been seen since the victory over the Axis nations in 1945—a growing belief that the United States is at the threshold of the "second American century" and can remake the world in its own image. Some experts are already confident that the United States will bring democracy to Iraq, solve the long-standing problems of the Middle East, and resolve the deep-rooted conflicts of the region.

Instead of being swept away by the notion that the Persian Gulf War heralds an era of prolonged, unquestioned U.S. dominance in world affairs, Americans should soberly assess that conflict and its implications. It is clear in retrospect that those who predicted a long struggle with thousands of American casualties were wrong. It is equally clear that the capability of Iraq's military apparatus was vastly overestimated by both supporters and opponents of the war. The reason for that overestimation is itself an extremely important question. There is a gnawing suspicion that the U.S. national security establishment may have deliberately hyped Iraq's military prowess both to justify the U.S. intervention and to magnify the significance of the subsequent victory. In any case, it is difficult to square the image of an army that performed so pathetically with Washington's propaganda barrage about a vaunted military machine capable of dominating the entire Middle East. Iraq's anemic performance supports the view that other powers in the region

1

had sufficient military capabilities of their own to stifle Baghdad's expansionism. Employing U.S. military power for that purpose was akin to using a sledgehammer to kill a gnat.

Although the debate about some of the narrow military issues has been resolved (predominantly in favor of the pro-war faction), most of the pertinent issues in the prewar debate have not vanished. Indeed, some of them may be more relevant than before. The implications of President Bush's vision of a "new world order," the probable impact of the gulf war on America's relations with the Islamic world, and the feasibility of future collective security enterprises, to name just a few topics, have acquired a new urgency.

The Cato Institute is proud to have held a conference that brought together an array of policy experts to address those and other important issues *before* the fighting erupted. That conference, "America in the Gulf: Vital Interests or Pointless Entanglement?" was held on January 8, 1991, in Washington, D.C. It represented a searching analysis of the course charted by President Bush—a course that led to war just eight days later. The essays in this collection are based on the papers presented at the conference. Some of the authors revised their essays in the week following the conference, but all revisions were completed before the start of Operation Desert Storm on January 16. The accuracy of the authors' prewar judgments, therefore, can be assessed in light of subsequent developments.

The United States needs to engage in a serious discussion of the significance of the Persian Gulf War. That policy postmortem should go beyond the initial euphoria about the military triumph to confront the Bush administration with a number of probing questions. The president should be asked to explain why the invasion of Kuwait made Saddam the equivalent of Hitler, but Iraq's earlier invasion of Iran and the flagrant use of chemical weapons did not. Indeed, he should be asked to explain why Washington actively assisted Iraq in its campaign against Iran, most prominently by sending U.S. naval forces to the Persian Gulf in 1987–88. (One must assume that, as vice president during those years, Bush was more than a passive observer when that myopic strategy was adopted.) The Bush administration's shifting justifications for a policy that led to war and the frequent gaps between its official positions and its actual conduct should also be scrutinized.

2

Finally, there must be a full national debate on the rationale for President Bush's new world order, the costs and risks of that strategy to the United States, and the possibility that the Persian Gulf intervention is to be a model for America's world role in the 1990s and the early 21st century. Before the Persian Gulf crisis erupted, an embryonic discussion was under way about the "peace dividend" America could anticipate from the end of the cold war. Proponents of a global interventionist strategy for the United States in the post-cold-war era have already seized on the gulf episode as a pretext for perpetuating the bloated U.S. military budget. Advocating either a crusade for global stability or global democracy (or in some cases both objectives, despite the inherent contradictions), they envisage a mission that would keep the military establishment busy—and generously funded—for decades to come. Those who believe that America has an opportunity to reap substantial benefits from the end of the cold war and that it should develop a security strategy based on a less expansive definition of American vital interests must engage proponents of a new world order in far-reaching debate.

The contributors to this collection address a variety of essential issues that will not vanish with the end of military operations in the Persian Gulf. The essays, therefore, can provide an important bridge between the prewar and postwar foreign policy debates.

Ted Galen Carpenter
March 1, 1991

Part I

The Context:
President Bush's New World Order

1. The Persian Gulf Crisis and the "New" World Order

Christopher Layne

Those who have called the Persian Gulf crisis the first worldwide crisis of the post-cold-war era are wrong. U.S. foreign policy is still very much driven by cold-war thinking—the same vision of "world-order" politics that has shaped policy since World War II. Instead of judiciously weighing America's tangible concerns in the crisis, the United States was dragged into the gulf by the dead weight of the cold war's intellectual baggage. During the post–World War II era, American decisionmakers adopted a fixed view of world politics and stock responses to global crises. Attempting to create a global environment compatible with America's politico-economic institutions and values, Washington emphasized the discriminating application of military power, "collective security," and U.S. political and economic intervention in other nations' internal affairs.[1] The Bush administration's reaction to Iraq's invasion of Kuwait was Pavlovian—a conditioned response right out of the cold-war era. U.S. policymakers did not stop to ask whether rote cold-war responses were relevant in a world where the political, military, and economic balance of forces was shifting dramatically.

In the final analysis, the United States was propelled into the Persian Gulf by the Bush administration's vision of a "new world order." From day one, Bush declared that Iraq's annexation of Kuwait would not stand. However, going to war to liberate Kuwait and restore its ruler—a semifeudal Middle Eastern potentate with a penchant for womanizing, gambling, and driving Rolls Royces— was not a winning domestic political hand. But by putting the Kuwaiti microstate's fate into a larger context, the administration believed it could sell its policy to the American people. Thus, Iraq's invasion of Kuwait became the test case—"the first assault on the new world we seek"—of whether the post-cold-war world would sink into anarchy or be governed by "an international order—a

7

common code and rule of law that promotes cooperation in place of conflict."[2] The new world order was more than a public relations gambit, however. It was the administration's response to the intellectual crisis in American foreign policy provoked by the cold war's end.

In 1945 the United States was the only superpower militarily and economically. However, the Soviet Union was formidable militarily, was aggressive ideologically, and appeared to threaten Western Europe and Japan. To prevent a possible adverse shift in the global balance, the United States protected those vulnerable, war-damaged countries while helping them regain political stability and prosperity. And in the Third World, the United States engaged in "nation building" to immunize newly independent ex-colonies against the virus of communist-supported wars of national liberation. The long-term U.S. aim was to restore a multipolar power balance so that Western Europe, Japan, and other friendly regional powers could assume primary responsibility for their own security. At the same time, it was hoped that the sustained pressure of containment would eventually transform the Soviet Union into a less ideological and less threatening great power.

Those objectives have been attained. Revolutionary change is sweeping the Soviet Union, which has been marginalized as a factor in world politics. Western Europe and Japan are solidly democratic and economically dynamic. Communism's collapse in East Central Europe and Germany's unification have ended Europe's division. The fading of the U.S.-Soviet rivalry has made the Third World largely irrelevant geopolitically. But a funny thing happened on the way to the post-cold-war era. Although the world changed, the world view of America's foreign policy establishment remained static. Perhaps that should not be surprising. For American internationalists, the conclusions that follow logically from the cold war's end are unacceptable. Admitting that the cold-war paradigm's basic assumptions—the Soviet threat, bipolarity, and U.S. economic predominance—had been demolished would necessitate a drastic change in American foreign policy, an adjustment to the changed conditions in international politics.

From that perspective, it is easy to understand why the American foreign policy elite continued to say the cold war was alive and well long past the time when it was obviously dead and buried.[3] Even the Bush administration was finally forced to acknowledge that the cold war had vanished into history's mists, but it wanted to perpetuate the cold-war paradigm and the American world role that rested on it. The response was to marginally alter the cold-war paradigm to make it appear that it was a new paradigm—one that accounted for phenomena that the old analytical framework could not explain. Thus, the cold-war paradigm metamorphosed into the new world order.

From 1945 until 1990, virtually every U.S. geopolitical initiative was justified by reference to the Soviet threat. For the new world order to be viable, American policymakers needed to find a substitute rationale for an active policy of global diplomatic and military engagement. Magically, a new threat materialized, summed up in the Bush administration's mantra of "uncertainty, instability, and danger."[4] According to the administration, in this uncertain, dangerous, and unstable new world, threats to American interests will not diminish even if Soviet geopolitical power does. As Gen. Colin Powell told the House Appropriations Committee, "Other threats to American interests do not disappear because of a retrenched Soviet Union."[5] Indeed, now we are told that the post-cold-war world will be a more dangerous place for the United States than the cold-war world was because of the proliferation of weapons of mass destruction in hostile states, anti-American regimes in the Third World, drug traffickers, anti-democratic insurgents, and terrorism.[6] In the face of those new dangers, it is said, the United States will have to be more, not less, interventionist.[7] The administration's geopolitical response to the cold war's end was succinct: "read our lips, no new thinking."

To replace the obsolete mission of containing the Soviet Union, American internationalists have declared that the new U.S. role is nothing less than preserving the "peace and stability of the world" in a new, more dangerous, and more uncertain era. The United States must resist aggression to ensure that "the rule of law supplants the rule of the jungle." The new world order requires that aggression be opposed everywhere and compromised with nowhere. That is the lesson of the 1930s, which Bush believes is still relevant: "If history teaches us anything, it is that we must resist aggression or it will destroy our freedoms. Appeasement does not work." The new world order is to be defended by collective security arrangements; nevertheless, there is no substitute for American leadership of the international community. Because the United States is the only remaining superpower, unique responsibilities are imposed on it. America, we are told, is "bound to lead."[8]

There is, however, nothing new about the Bush administration's "new" world order. It differs from the old world order (embodied in the Truman and Reagan doctrines and the foreign policy of the Kennedy and Johnson administrations) only in a minor semantic aspect. The old world order was based on the perceived need to oppose communism worldwide. In the new world order, the need "to fight aggression and preserve the sovereignty of nations" has replaced the vanished communist threat. Both rest on the ostensible lessons of Munich: that peace is indivisible, that aggression must be resisted everywhere, and that totalitarian dictators are insatiably expansionist. Thus, central to the concept of world-order politics is the notion that America's overseas commitments are a seamless web. Consequently, any failure to oppose a transgression of the world order's behavioral norms will produce a dominolike chain reaction. As Bush argued in explaining his Persian Gulf policy, if the United States had "not responded to this first provocation [Iraq's invasion of Kuwait] with clarity of purpose, if we do not continue to demonstrate our determination, it would be a signal to actual and potential despots around the world."[9]

World order—new and old—requires the United States to take the lead in organizing the international community to resist those who would dare to disturb the peace. In short, the world-order thinking that led the United States into the Persian Gulf is exactly the same kind of thinking that led America into disaster in Vietnam. As ex-secretary of state Dean Rusk admits in his memoirs, the belief that America was responsible for ensuring global stability by stopping aggression everywhere and upholding international law underlay U.S. policy in Vietnam—another Wilsonian crusade fought largely alone by the United States (as a Persian Gulf war would be) in the name of collective security. In Rusk's words:

> The overriding problem for us in Southeast Asia was the same problem that all mankind faces: how to prevent World War III. The principal lesson I learned from World War II was that if aggression is allowed to gather momentum, it can continue to build and lead to general war. That is why

10

we drafted the United Nations Charter and the collective security treaties of the postwar period. If I thought there was no connection between the events in Southeast Asia, the broad structure of world peace, and the possibility of a third world war, I might have advised differently on Vietnam. But in Southeast Asia, and in that pattern of aggression practiced by North Vietnam, I saw what I thought were the seeds of conflict for future wars.[10]

The Persian Gulf intervention is a reminder that U.S. policy is shaped less by deterministic forces than by choice. Internationalists' commitment to world-order politics reflects their world view and their values. However, their policy choices do not have to be America's. They hold on to world-order politics because they cannot envision—or will not accept—an American post-cold-war role that differs significantly from the cold-war role.

National interest realism, Hans Morgenthau said, is a concept that should save the United States from "moral excess and political folly"—both of which are abundantly present in America's Persian Gulf policy.[11] Faithful to the ethic of responsibility, realists ask questions about the consequences of Washington's gulf policy that internationalists leave unanswered. What would be the scope and intensity of a U.S.-Iraqi war? How would the conflict be terminated? What would its effect be on Middle Eastern politics? On U.S. relations with Western Europe and Japan?

But realists see the Persian Gulf crisis in a larger context, too: will American foreign policy be based on old myths or on new realities? To be sure, the internationalists are right. If the United States elects to do so, it can stick with world-order politics for some time. But while internationalists are strong on policy preferences, they are weak on policy consequences. In fact, they deny that their policy has any negative consequences. For example, when pushed, they admit that U.S. power has declined, but they deny that the decline has any practical implication for American foreign policy. As Deputy Secretary of State Lawrence S. Eagleburger put it, "The shift in the balance of power among the leading Western countries does not mean the U.S. must abandon its leadership role."[12] Internationalists are also weak on values. They take a statist position that regards America's citizens, resources, and institutions as existing only for the purpose of supporting world order's pretensions. They argue that democratic institutions inhibit the conduct of a super-power's foreign policy, and they claim that America's strength is eroding not because of its overseas commitments but because Americans live too well.[13]

Realists see things differently. America can choose the course of world-order politics, but the consequence will be an accelerated decline as national resources are frittered away on overseas cru-sades. Realists believe that the United States can abandon world-order politics without endangering national interests and that the United States can choose to retrench abroad in order to stimulate renewal at home. In the realists' hierarchy of values, the purpose of foreign policy is to ensure the nation's safety precisely so its citizens can enjoy the good life: individual freedom of choice, the fruits of a free and dynamic economy, and the ordered liberty of democratic government.

The Bush administration sees itself as heir to the tradition of the "wise men" who shaped post–World War II U.S. policy. But the Bush administration is foreign policy's Milli Vanilli: it is simply lip-syncing the words sung by the world-order lyricists of the Truman and Reagan doctrines and the Vietnam War. Such a cold-war mind-set has little applicability to the new international system now taking shape. The administration's songs belong to a long-gone era. As Sidney Blumenthal observes, "The prevailing concepts of Cold War politics—appeasement, containment, falling dominoes—were rooted in the understanding of the generation that had fought World War II."[14] That generation and its ideas have overstayed their welcome on history's stage. The United States can no longer afford a foreign policy that ossified intellectually somewhere between Munich and Vietnam. A "new paradigm" is needed even more urgently in foreign policy than it is in domestic policy.

Notes

The research assistance of John Butler is gratefully acknowledged.

[1]Patrick Hatcher lists these as the basic strategies through which post–World War II internationalists implemented their globalist approach to American foreign policy. See Patrick Hatcher, *The Suicide of an Elite: American Internationalists and Vietnam* (Stanford, Calif.: Stanford University Press, 1990), pp. 3–31 and *passim*.

[2]George Bush, "Against Aggression in the Persian Gulf" and "Toward a New World Order," *Current Policy*, nos. 1293 and 1298 (Washington: U.S. Department of State), August 15, 1990, and September 11, 1990.

³See, for example, Richard M. Nixon, "American Foreign Policy: The Bush Agenda," *Foreign Affairs* 68, no. 1 (Winter 1988/89): 199–219. As late as July 1990—after the Soviets had accepted a reunified Germany as a full NATO member—Henry Kissinger was still warning that the West was allowing itself to be "mesmerized" by Gorbachev to the detriment of NATO's cohesion. Henry A. Kissinger, "As Gorbachev Mesmerizes, Is the Atlantic Alliance Perhaps Sleeping?" *Los Angeles Times*, July 22, 1990, p. M2.

⁴As Bush stated in a May 4, 1990, speech at Oklahoma State University, "You see, our enemy today—if you think about it, what's the enemy today—our enemy is uncertainty and instability." As General Powell told the Veterans of Foreign Wars on August 23, 1990: "But it's a changing not a changed world. It's a world full of instability, uncertainty and danger."

⁵As Secretary of Defense Richard Cheney told Congress in 1990, "Regardless of whether Soviet military power diminishes, many U.S. allies will continue to face major threats." Statement of Secretary of Defense Richard Cheney before the Senate Budget Committee, February 5, 1990; statement of Secretary of Defense Richard Cheney to the Senate Appropriations Committee, June 12, 1990. Interestingly, the Pentagon still clings to the old cold-war paradigm, with some subtle changes. Now, rather than the prospect of Soviet aggression, it is the "uncertainty of the Soviet Union's domestic and international future" that militates against any changes in the U.S. military posture. Ibid. See also Secretary of Defense Cheney's briefing on DOD's fiscal year 1991 budget and General Powell's statement (February 8, 1990) to the defense subcommittee of the House Appropriations Committee: "The Soviet Union will remain a military superpower. . . . It is still too soon to make sweeping changes to strategy, force structure and posture, and modernization."

⁶Ibid.

⁷See, for example, "From Abyss to Brink: Will the United States Be More Interventionist in a Post–Cold War World?" *Newsweek*, January 8, 1990.

⁸The quotations are from three Bush speeches that outline the basis of the new world order: "Against Aggression in the Persian Gulf"; "Toward a New World Order"; "The Arabian Peninsula: U.S. Principles," *Current Policy*, no. 1292, August 8, 1990. Also see Secretary Baker's statement, "America's Stake in the Persian Gulf Crisis," *Current Policy*, no. 1297, September 4, 1990. In a March 23, 1990, Los Angeles speech, General Powell said: "We are a superpower. At the moment, in many respects, we are the only superpower in each of the critical aspects of power. . . . Superpower status imposes responsibilities on us. Our outlook must be global and it must encompass the strong alliances that are critical to the future peace of the world. . . . America must lead the world into the 21st century, if it is to be a century of peace." Colin Powell, "U.S. Foreign Policy in a Changing World: Keeping Democracy Alive," *Vital Speeches*, May 1, 1990. In his August 1990 address to the VFW, Powell said: "It is the reality that America is the only superpower left in all the dimensions of power—political, economic, military, and the power of our values. And that reality creates another enduring need—the need for world leadership. We cannot shrink from it. America must be a leader."

⁹George Bush, "Toward a New World Order."

¹⁰Dean Rusk, *As I Saw It* (New York: W. W. Norton, 1990), pp. 494–95. Rusk also states his view "that the integrity of the U.S. commitment was the principal pillar

13

of peace in the world [and] that the Communist world might draw the wrong conclusions that could lead to world war if we reneged on our commitments." As he explains: "My generation of students was led down the path into the catastrophe of World War II, which could have been prevented. We came out of that war thinking that collective security was the key to the prevention of World War III." Ibid., pp. 450, 503.

[11]Quoted in Michael Joseph Smith, *Realist Thought from Weber to Kissinger* (Baton Rouge: Louisiana State University Press, 1986), p. 147.

[12]Lawrence S. Eagleburger, "Uncharted Waters: U.S. Foreign Policy in a Time of Transition," speech delivered at Georgetown University, September 13, 1989.

[13]See Samuel P. Huntington, "The U.S.—Decline or Renewal?" *Foreign Affairs* 67, no. 2 (Winter 1988–89), pp. 87–88.

[14]Sidney Blumenthal, *Pledging Allegiance: The Last Campaign of the Cold War* (New York: Harper & Collins, 1990), p. 154.

2. The Continuing Need for U.S. Leadership

Robert E. Hunter

The end of the cold war has provided a time for reflection about the future of U.S. foreign policy. Not unnaturally, the last year or so has been a time of extremes, pitting those who wish the United States to search for opportunities to continue pursuing a central role as superpower—fortuitously no longer opposed by a near equal—against those who believe that the American people can now retreat into themselves, "tending their gardens," with at most a bit of dabbling in the Western Hemisphere.

That is, of course, a caricature of both positions, but it is instructive in showing the extent to which predilection can prevail over analysis—or simple common sense. And it is here that examination should begin. Indeed, setting a course for the American future in the outside world should start with the facts and proceed to key choices.

The most immediate fact promoting a reassessment of the U.S. role in the world is that the United States has, for the third time in this century, emerged victorious from a global conflict. Indeed, it is better positioned than any other significant power. Its gross national product is unparalleled and still accounts for close to one-quarter of worldwide wealth. (For the "declinists" among us, it should be noted that that is the classic pattern of the past century, save for the unusual circumstances following the economic catastrophe that befell other countries in World War II.) While now being outpaced in terms of rate of increase, U.S. productivity is still the highest in the world. Today the United States faces no "natural" enemies, no direct threats to the homeland, including the threat of nuclear war. Indeed, one of the major miracles of all time is that the world escaped the prospect of its second and final nuclear war. Even in the one area that most changed U.S. geopolitical circumstances during the early 1950s—the loss of the sanctuary provided by two broad oceans—the United States has reclaimed its past status, at least in the politics of threat from the Soviet Union if not in its practical possibilities of threat (the continued existence of the Soviet nuclear arsenal).

At the same time, however, the United States has lost the ability to stand aloof from the world. Isolationism, as a statement of psychology, politics, and economics, has effectively come to an end. That fact is now increasingly recognized in the United States, following a decade during which top U.S. leadership tried to indulge a national flight from this reality. The Federal Reserve does not have a monopoly on setting the value of the dollar; the Texas Railroad Commission, the price of oil; or the Mercantile Exchange, the price of food. Every several hours, more currency is traded in international commerce, beyond the control of central banks, than is in the annual U.S. government budget. U.S. jobs, investment, productivity, sales, and income now depend—in sector after sector—on what happens abroad as well as what happens at home.

All that is now child's play, a reality that is as near as the closest television monitor or satellite hookup. Reality, and its allied political and cultural phenomena, can be seen in the spread of ideas beyond national control and in the technological and ideological basis of the global earthquake that will forever be known as 1989.

The logic of those statements argues that the United States is now living in a world dominated by economics more than ever before— a world where the risks of war have declined, where military power is less relevant, and where ideas and their propagation have taken on not a new importance (that has always been true) but a priority less challenged by what are considered classical forms of power and influence. But does that justify an abrupt change in U.S. attitudes toward the outside world, an abdication of leadership, a retreat from responsibilities, and an inward-looking approach that will, perhaps, make America an "ordinary" nation?

There is risk in the ensuing debate of pitting ideological positions against one another, of confusing in confrontation at least two forms of nostalgia born of different historical myths: those of American self-sufficiency of the interwar years and those of American preeminence through most of the cold-war era. Neither paradigm has much validity for the future.

The Persian Gulf crisis offers an opportunity to look at America's potential role in the world in terms of practical cases. The opportunity exists at several levels, each of which is worthy of discussion far beyond what is permitted here. The following are some of the early "lessons" of the current crisis that are relevant.

Most obvious—and most comforting to a view of the relevance of U.S. power—on August 3 no other state in the world was prepared to act to counter Iraq's aggression against Kuwait and, potentially, against Saudi Arabia. Perhaps the latter threat was fantasy; but so too, a few days earlier, seemed a potential Iraqi threat to Kuwait, as viewed by many people in many countries who should have known better. Principle number one, therefore, can be discussed in terms of who will act. Of course, that statement begs the questions of act for what? and how? and why? Those are all legitimate questions. But the fact remains that, a week or two weeks or a month after Iraq's invasion, other countries would still have been asking the questions, whereas the United States was prepared to do something.

Nevertheless, in the post-cold-war era, it is not obvious that the United States should automatically or regularly assume responsibility for being the principal "actor," even when a collection of countries concludes that there is a common interest in doing something in one part of the world or another. Obviously, as well, part of the challenge for the United States is encouraging other states to accept more responsibility—including a role in defining the concept of "responsibility" in particular circumstances. Major parts of the agenda—in the West—were clear well before the end of the cold war. During several administrations, the United States was reluctant to accept and acknowledge a growing role in foreign policy for the European Community, as such—although the Bush administration has now picked up where the Carter administration left off in supporting the European Community. For some time it has been clear that the United States has a final task, indeed responsibility, left over from World War II, regarding Japan and Germany. That task is to help them progress from being major global economic powers to being major global political powers, but with a historically unprecedented difference: to do so without their becoming major military powers (in Germany's case, in large part by submerging it in the European Community).

In part, therefore, the issue today for the United States is one of transition and authority. How well and how fast are we prepared to devolve at least some responsibility (where that can be agreed to) on other nations? How well and how fast are they prepared to accept it? And as a nation, how far are we prepared to share responsibilities—that is, to accept with others a "fair share" of common action, whether in the West, smaller coalitions, or the United Nations—without our also having to dominate decision-making and influence? The answer to that last question is particularly unclear, but its implication—that abandoning a leadership role is not necessarily America's current destiny—must not be dismissed out of hand. Nations do have vocations, at particular moments in history, and we need to understand and decide what vocation to have for the near future. Perhaps it is leadership in the West and more broadly (for which we have a record, though blemished, that compares well historically). Or perhaps, in the view of some Americans, our vocation is a continuing role in the Middle East that derives from the earlier imperialism of Britain and France, but for which, culturally and politically, we have no aptitude and vocation.

At the same time, the appeal of sharing responsibility and developing elements of leadership should not be interpreted as meaning that the United States should exercise no leadership and simply retreat. Some leadership will simply be "thrust upon" us by dint of our size, power, and engagement—for instance, in the management of the global economy. Some will accrue from a list of issues from which our abstention would thwart effective response and our inability to form a politically cohesive response could doom others' efforts to failure. (That situation is likely to be true, in particular, with regard to the four major global challenges of the next century: proliferation, pollution, population, and poverty.)

The list of new global challenges is also important in posing the question, "leadership for what?" In the post-cold-war era, the United States has a chance—indeed, a responsibility—to view its engagement in the outside world in terms that will provide benefits for a wider group of people and nations than ever before. In the absence of a transcending threat to national security, there is an opportunity to define "security"—as well as "interests"—much more broadly. Those definitions will be critical, not just to validate any role of the United States for its own citizens but also to create a moral basis for action abroad. The shift in leadership will require a profound change in national attitude, but it is consistent with U.S. national ideals.

The current crisis also pricks the balloon of one fantasy that emerged from the end of the cold war: that the role of military power had not just been depreciated—true, at least in Central Europe—but that it had become largely irrelevant, universally. That was part of the "end of history" illusion, where an essay became, briefly, an ideology, thus betraying a Western cultural bias. Interstate conflict, like other aspects of life, could have no meaning if it did not deeply engage the first and second worlds. (Just as suffering and death associated with wars in Ethiopia-Eritrea and Iran-Iraq did not resonate particularly in the West—they were not about "history," meaning the destiny of the West.)

By the same token, the Persian Gulf crisis has changed perspectives on the use of force. For example, it is doubtful that Iraq would have attacked Kuwait if the cold war were continuing, considering that previously the superpowers had been willing to exercise discipline on their respective client states in regions where conflict between states could lead to conflict between superpowers (in speeches during 1990, Saddam Hussein showed awareness of that factor). Also, in theory, the United States is now in a position to use as much force as it chooses in most of what has been called the Third World, in any way it pleases, without let or hindrance. In fact, however, it has made an unprecedented use of the United Nations—admittedly aided by two developments: the changed attitude of the Soviet Union and the need to keep Iraq from representing the crisis as pitting a champion of the Arab masses against the "imperialists and Zionists" (Saddam's words). Likewise, for reasons that can only be a combination of the moral and the political, there has been no contemplation of the use of the U.S. nuclear arsenal, even if such use would not provoke escalation. And the U.S. government has found itself in a situation where it can, if it is wise, actually abide by the dicta of Karl Maria von Clausewitz, the nonpareil of modern strategy, to pursue a political end by the most judicious use of military power—namely, its nonuse.

The political and economic causes for which the United States will become involved abroad have also come under scrutiny. During the cold war, there was—for good or ill—a settled policy: George Kennan might complain that he was misinterpreted, but the nation went on with a basic adherence to a policy of containment. The rest, in retrospect, was tactics. Vietnam, the most expensive "tactical" error, was debated in the United States largely in terms of its relevance to a broader consideration of the conduct of the cold war. Even most of the moral propositions about the U.S. role in that war made obeisance to the larger moral construct, well or badly conceived.

In the Persian Gulf today, there is no such settled policy, and thus, there can be no easy domestic debate about war. At the same time, the resolution of the current crisis—especially the resolution of the philosophical and political debate in the United States about the use of force—cannot have universal application in the post-cold-war era. Right now, barring either a sudden emergence of an aggressive China or a recrudescence of Soviet authority, military cohesion, and ambition, there can be no contemplation of major military threats to U.S. interests. In addition, no spot on earth is of interest to so many countries as the Persian Gulf is—no spot whatsoever. On the face of it, therefore, the current crisis is not a precedent for future U.S. engagements or for tomorrow's structure of international relations (beyond the new widespread deference to the United Nations), unless we strain credulity by extrapolating from current circumstances to "fighting the last war" in terms of lessons seemingly learned in the Persian Gulf.

Furthermore, while the United States has a long-term strategic interest in the Persian Gulf, at the moment at least, no specific vital interest in the region is directly at risk (e.g., something worth fighting for under the terms of the so-called Weinberger Doctrine, which accurately defined the historic U.S. attitude to war: that the objective of conflict must be vital, and the war must have the backing of the American people; that allies should be engaged if possible; and that the United States should use sufficient power, use it rapidly and effectively, and win). The only vital interest put specifically at risk in this crisis was the need to contain Iraq, and that has been done; the only other interest for which the average American would be prepared to fight was securing the freedom of U.S. hostages, and that has been done. The rest is secondary, not worth a single American life, especially when there are nonmilitary

20

(economic and political) means to achieve the same objectives of containing, repelling, and trammelling Iraq and its military power. Those objectives still must be met, however, and that, along with helping to create some system of regional security—one that severely limits any U.S. military power that could stimulate negative reactions—will require major U.S. leadership efforts.

Nevertheless, that limitation on the validity of using U.S. military force in the current Persian Gulf crisis must not be misinterpreted to mean either that (1) there is no further relevance of military power or (2) the United States should leave it to others rather than share it with others. On the first point, after the cold war, the world is now clearly a much safer place, with the rapid decline in the threat of global nuclear war (even though the risk of regional nuclear war continues to be significant). But it is far from clear that there will be an absence of stress and tension in parts of the world where the United States and other countries have an interest, if only in securing some economic benefit, such as the flow of oil. Fortunately, in the Persian Gulf today, we can slow down the process of decision; indeed, the rush to January 15 has no relationship either to the issues at stake or to necessary crisis tactics. And we have the luxury—unprecedented in the post–World War II era with an issue of such magnitude—of putting matters into perspective, choosing instruments of power and influence (many or mostly nonmilitary), and counting both the costs and the moral dimensions. The decline of the cold war mandates a decline in the impetus to U.S. imperialism, even as it makes its pursuit theoretically more possible.

The second point—the role of others—relates directly to the renewed issue of burden sharing. That concept, of course, implies a settled agreement on what burdens are to be shared. Today that is far from clear, despite the general allied fellowship under U.S. leadership in the Persian Gulf crisis. In traditional U.S. relations with allies such as Japan and the West European states, there is tacit agreement, at least for the time being, to let sleeping dogs lie. That is, if there are no threats to core interests (from the Soviet Union or China), why disturb settled relationships for the sake of change? Change will come, of course. But there has been no great impetus for changing abruptly or for mandating a reduction in U.S. political engagement in Europe or Asia, even if—especially on

Continental issues—there is a progressive decline in U.S. bargaining influence in nonmilitary areas because the military relevance of the U.S. presence is declining.

The Persian Gulf crisis is waking up some of those dogs. It has raised the hoary issue of the competence of the Western alliance "outside the area"—that is, beyond the strict confines (mandated by the United States!) of the North Atlantic Treaty. It has brought into play the thorny issues of the Arab-Israeli conflict, on which there has rarely been transatlantic agreement. It has brought Europeans so quickly after the end of the cold war to worry again about U.S. attitudes toward the use of force, especially when European interests might be adversely affected. And it has produced strains in the United States about the sharing of burdens in two respects: budgetary impact and the potential loss of life in war. From the European perspective, generalized, the United States can be entrusted with the lead—indeed, no one else wants it!—but the United States also needs wise counsel from its transatlantic cousins. From a U.S. government perspective, once again America's allies do not understand the validity of U.S. concepts of truth and justice. The two perspectives are a recipe for a classical misunderstanding, but more to the point, they set the stage for a future redefinition of transatlantic common interests now that two things have happened: (1) the Russian bear—at least for the time being—seems to have gone back to his lair and (2) the United States sees its own blood and treasure at stake in a part of the world where other states have a greater commercial interest, but where there is no basic Soviet dimension that needs to be "managed" by the competent Western superpower.

That point brings us back to the start of this essay and provides some practical conclusions about at least the next few years. Like it or not, the Persian Gulf remains a vital strategic interest of the United States. But other countries must share the burden, and we must be smart about what we do: a permanent U.S. military presence is likely to cause more problems than it solves.

From a broader perspective, it is clear that the United States will continue to have objectives to pursue in the outside world; that the security of some of those objectives could require the employment of military power; and that the United States will need to be judicious in deciding where its interests are engaged, what the best instruments are, and whom it should seek to be involved with it. It is clear that the United States should develop coalitions with different countries for different purposes, with a sharing of burdens depending on the quality and aspect of the matter to be addressed. Clearly, America needs to consider the extent to which it needs to be "in charge" of decisions made about issues affecting its destiny, as opposed to sharing decisionmaking as the price of collective action. And it is clear that the United States will need to consider, on its own and with allies, the underlying and unspoken questions of national ambition and vocation—in a word, the issue of leadership. Abdication of responsibility and leadership are not compatible concepts; devolution of responsibility and leadership can be, provided that there is someone else ready and able to share in taking up the slack—indeed, in defining what common goals there may be. That, however, is more the stuff of history than of politics.

3. Washington's Collective Security Facade

Ted Galen Carpenter

Washington's Persian Gulf policy has been characterized by an assortment of self-serving illusions, suggesting either a lack of analysis or a lack of intellectual honesty on the part of U.S. policymakers. The gap between the Bush administration's interpretation of events and the underlying reality is apparent in many ways. The administration's justifications for the intervention have been rambling, inconsistent, and unconvincing, seemingly motivated more by shifting estimates of the argument that would attract the most domestic support than by any coherent policy rationale.

A similar sense of unreality pervades the matching of means and ends. In particular, it is highly unlikely that the administration's "maximalist" objectives—a complete and unconditional Iraqi withdrawal from Kuwait and the elimination of Baghdad's embryonic nuclear capability—can be achieved without massive and costly military operations against the Iraqi homeland to replace the current government with a more pliant regime. Yet despite an increasing emphasis on those maximalist goals in recent weeks, administration leaders insist that they hope to avoid war.

It might be possible to gain some Iraqi concessions, including perhaps a withdrawal from most Kuwaiti territory, through diplomacy. But "sending Saddam Hussein back to Baghdad with his tail between his legs," as Secretary of Defense Richard Cheney put it so quaintly; hinting that Nuremberg-style war-crimes trials await Saddam and his associates; and stating that unspecified measures (probably the continuation of the economic blockade) will be used to degrade Iraq's military capability, even if Baghdad complies fully with the UN resolutions, constitute the functional equivalent of a demand for unconditional surrender. When Bush administration officials imply that such a humiliating capitulation can be obtained without war, either they are being naive or they think the American public is gullible.

The most striking example of the gap between illusion and reality, however, is the administration's repeated portrayal of the Persian Gulf operation as a bona fide collective security enterprise. President Bush never tires of asserting that the confrontation is "the world versus Saddam Hussein" and that 28 nations have military forces deployed in the gulf region to thwart Iraqi aggression. The creation of an international coalition in support of Washington's stance is a superficially impressive diplomatic ploy, but it lacks meaningful substance. In reality, the "collective security" effort is an overwhelmingly U.S. operation concealed by a barely credible international diplomatic facade: a Potemkin village collective security enterprise.

Although an array of governments have expressed support for economic and military sanctions against Iraq, as reflected in the decisive votes of the UN Security Council, their support rarely extends beyond the diplomatic realm, where the costs and risks are quite low. When it comes to sharing the financial burdens of the operation, the commitments are more tentative. And when it comes to sharing the risk of combat, several major powers (most notably, Germany and Japan) are conspicuous by their absence.

Monetarily, the United States has shouldered a significant percentage of the burden, and despite vague pledges of additional support from the Saudi monarchy and the emir of Kuwait, it will continue to do so. Washington's allies have thus far pledged approximately $9.7 billion in cash, equipment, and services to help defray the cost of military operations in the gulf.[1] But the Pentagon concedes that the cost of those operations may exceed $20 billion in fiscal year 1991, and most private estimates place the figure at more than $30 billion. Moreover, such estimates assume that the crisis will not explode into combat, a development that could cause expenses to reach $500 million to $1 billion per *day*.[2] When placed in that context, the allies' financial contributions seem quite modest.

U.S. dominance is more evident in the more serious matter of risk sharing. American military personnel account for more than 70 percent of the outside (i.e., non-Saudi) forces in the "international" force confronting Saddam. When the second-stage U.S. deployment is complete in late January or early February, the total will be more than 80 percent. At that point, the United States will have approximately 430,000 troops deployed; the next largest contingents will be those of Egypt (30,000–35,000), Britain (30,000), Syria (18,000), and France (15,000). Such contributions are little more than tokenism, and the deployments of the other allies hardly constitute even token support.

If fighting breaks out, the disparity may be even greater. Some Egyptian and Syrian officials have indicated that their forces will not be available for offensive operations inside Iraq, and U.S. military commanders have expressed skepticism about the usefulness or reliability of other allied forces under combat conditions. There is little doubt that U.S. troops would bear the brunt of any fighting and would probably suffer 80 percent or more of the casualties.

Despite the administration's propaganda, the Persian Gulf operation is not a genuine collective security effort. It is a policy formulated by Washington and implemented by U.S. military personnel. As a paradigm of post-cold-war international cooperation to carry out President Bush's vision of a "new world order," the operation is fraudulent. In fact, the first post-cold-war collective security enterprise bears a striking resemblance to the UN police action in Korea during the early stages of the cold war. President Harry S Truman and his advisers went to great lengths to portray that operation as a concerted effort of all peace-loving nations to repel aggression. But the Korean intervention was actually an outgrowth of intense U.S.-Soviet rivalry and was viewed by U.S. officials as an integral part of Washington's global strategy to contain Soviet power. Important policy decisions were made in Washington, not UN headquarters. The United States also provided approximately 85 percent of the "UN" forces and suffered nearly 90 percent of the casualties.[3]

The Korean intervention was not the only case in which Washington used a multilateral facade to conceal a U.S. operation for U.S. goals. Indeed, American leaders employed that stratagem throughout the cold war. Policymakers attempted to portray the Vietnam intervention as an international undertaking, touting the military contributions, meager though they were, made by South Korea and other U.S. clients. The Reagan administration did not intervene unilaterally in Lebanon in 1982; it did so as the leader of a "multinational peace-keeping force." Even the invasion of Grenada was not officially a U.S. action. American troops went into combat supposedly at the request of the previously obscure Organization of Eastern Caribbean States, and token paramilitary units from OECS member states went ashore with U.S. forces.[4]

Just as Washington's initial decision to intervene in the gulf crisis was based on obsolete cold-war assumptions (e.g., America has vital interests everywhere that must be defended; the United States is the only power capable of containing an aggressor), the strategy for carrying out that intervention was inherited from the cold war.[5] The Bush administration uses the illusion of a collective security effort to support its argument that Iraq is an international outlaw and to distract the American people from a disagreeable fact: American soldiers, not British, French, Egyptian, or Syrian—much less German, Italian, or Japanese—will suffer most of the casualties in a Persian Gulf war.

Even the most elaborate facade, however, cannot conceal reality: credible, *substantive* international support for the Persian Gulf operation is lacking, and populations throughout the Arab (indeed, the entire Islamic) world regard the intervention as a manifestation of U.S. imperialism. Both factors should counsel Washington to reconsider its strategy while there is still time to avert a tragedy.

The meager contributions of the Arab allies, the members of the European Community, and the Japanese are not merely an example of "free riding," although that undoubtedly plays a role. They also suggest that other governments do not accept the Bush administration's thesis that Saddam is another Hitler who poses a threat of global proportions. Instead, the other members of the international coalition seem to view Iraqi expansionism as a limited, regional threat—a perception that is far more accurate than Washington's hysterical exaggeration. As an abstract proposition, they would probably like to see Saddam's power curtailed, but they are unenthusiastic about waging a major war to do so. The surge in diplomatic activity by various members of the European Community in an attempt to find a political solution before the January 15 UN deadline is merely one indication of growing European uneasiness about the Bush administration's bellicosity. (The continuing efforts by Algerian president Chadli Bendjedid and other Arab leaders to formulate an acceptable compromise likewise highlight the concern of at least some Arab countries.) It is unlikely that major European and Middle Eastern powers (given their military capabilities and their apparent stake in halting Baghdad's expansionism) would be making only token military contributions and frantically seeking to avert a conflict if they thought the Iraqi threat was as grave as Bush alleges.

Although some Americans may accept the administration's contention that the gulf intervention is a noble international effort to defeat aggression, significant portions of the Islamic world are likely to see matters differently. The reaction of Arab populations to a U.S.-Iraqi war—especially to the spectacle of the United States, Israel's principal patron, killing Iraqi soldiers and civilians—would hardly be favorable. Indeed, the negative reaction might be severe enough to sweep away moderate, generally pro-U.S. regimes that have, at best, a tenuous hold on power. There have already been sizable anti-U.S. demonstrations in Jordan, Tunisia, and Sudan, and there are indications of serious opposition in Egypt, Syria, Turkey, and other regional allies to the willingness of the incumbent governments to embrace Washington's policy.

A prolonged U.S. military presence in the gulf following a conflict with Iraq would further entangle the United States in the intractable quarrels of that volatile region. Because of its previous cynical meddling (overthrowing the elected government of Iran in 1953 and intervening in the internal affairs of Lebanon in the early 1980s, to mention just two incidents), Washington does not have a very savory reputation in most portions of the Middle East. A new wave of interference would be viewed as additional evidence of U.S. imperialism and would make the United States a lightning rod for the anger and frustration of Pan-Arab nationalist and Islamic fundamentalist factions. Such dangers cannot be avoided by creating a collective security facade that has scant credibility. Yet there is little evidence that the administration considered those problems when it made the decision to intervene, and there is no indication that it now has a coherent strategy for dealing with them.

Instead, U.S. officials assure the American people that if a war against Iraq becomes necessary, a massive application of military force will secure a rapid and decisive victory. The possibility that U.S. forces may have to occupy Iraq; somehow set up a viable, nonthreatening Iraqi government; prevent other expansionist powers from exploiting the situation to advance their own agendas; and parry the hostility of outraged populations throughout the region is (perhaps understandably) never mentioned. The failure to discuss those less palatable scenarios reflects either an egregious lack of awareness of the dangers or a deliberate effort to mislead the American public.

Washington's Persian Gulf intervention is an ill-conceived policy with more than a small potential for disaster. President Bush is leading a divided nation into war in pursuit of vaguely defined objectives that have little relevance to America's vital interests—a conflict that may create far more problems than it could ever solve. Instead of fostering a host of self-serving illusions to rationalize a flawed strategy—especially the illusion that the intervention is a bona fide international effort to prevent aggression—the administration should encourage the concerned powers in the region to reach a peaceful compromise solution to the crisis and begin to extricate American forces from the Persian Gulf quagmire.

Notes

[1] Use of the vague term "services" to describe some of the contributions may mean that the allies are providing even less than the $9.7 billion figure implies. Nations that host U.S. forces have traditionally employed a variety of such gimmicks to magnify the extent of their support. For example, in the late 1980s the government of South Korea supposedly spent approximately $1.8 billion per year to help offset the cost of stationing U.S. troops in that country. A closer examination revealed that $1.5 billion consisted of "rent-free real estate." That "contribution" was based on the incredible proposition that American taxpayers should pay rent for the privilege of defending South Korea and that Seoul was doing them a favor by forgoing such charges. See Ted Galen Carpenter, "Beyond U.S. Paternalism: A New Security Strategy for the Pacific Basin," in *An American Vision: Policies for the '90s*, ed. Edward H. Crane and David Boaz (Washington: Cato Institute, 1989), pp. 175–76. Since the Pentagon has often collaborated in such deception, Americans should be on the lookout for evidence that a similar "shell game" is being played with Persian Gulf burden sharing.

[2] Rick Atkinson, "Costs of Confrontation: Who Pays? How Much?" *Washington Post*, August 18, 1990, p. A1. The larger figure assumes the need to replace items in the Pentagon's arsenal that would be destroyed in a gulf war. Theoretically, the U.S. military could simply absorb such losses, on the assumption that with the end of the cold war full replenishment would not be necessary. Such a reaction from the Pentagon bureaucracy is, however, rather unlikely.

[3] The *New York Times* noted that the European allies "are contributing about the same proportion of troops to the gulf today that they sent to fight in Korea in the early 1950s, when their economies were in tatters and their interests distant." "Who Will Pay for the Gulf Crisis?" (editorial), *New York Times*, October 8, 1990, p. A12.

⁴For a discussion of the U.S. tendency to cloak unilateral initiatives in threadbare multilateral garb throughout the cold war, see Ted Galen Carpenter, "Direct Military Intervention," in *Intervention in the 1980s: U.S. Foreign Policy in the Third World*, ed. Peter J. Schraeder (Boulder, Colo.: Lynne Rienner Publishers, 1989), pp. 131–46.

⁵For discussions of the Bush administration's Persian Gulf policy as a Pavlovian response inherited from the cold-war era, see Ted Galen Carpenter, "Bush Jumped the Gun in the Gulf," *New York Times*, August 18, 1990, p. A25, and Christopher Layne and Ted Galen Carpenter, "Arabian Nightmares: Washington's Persian Gulf Entanglement," Cato Institute Policy Analysis, no. 142, November 9, 1990.

4. A European View on the Gulf Crisis

Peter Riddell

Late last September Robert Zoellick, State Department counselor
and one of the central architects of the Bush administration's European policy, raised the question of whether the new post-cold-war
Europe would be "insular, itinerant or international." He naturally
hoped, and believed, that the new Europe would be international
and would continue to work together in rejuvenated or new
arrangements with the United States and Japan.

But the Persian Gulf crisis has raised doubts about that hope.
Europe—that is, most countries apart from Britain—has taken a
different view of the crisis than has the United States. I want to
explore the nature of those differences, the reasons for them, and
the implications for U.S.-European relations.

Any talk of a common European view has to be heavily qualified.
The 12 foreign ministers of the European Community may meet
together frequently, coordinate their actions through the European
political cooperation structure, and issue joint statements. But indi-
vidually they still pursue separate foreign policies and have taken
distinct views of the gulf crisis. Only two countries, Britain and
France, have committed ground troops to Saudi Arabia, and only
British forces are integrated under U.S. command. Several countries
have sent naval forces to enforce the trade embargo and have
recently sent aircraft to Turkey under separate NATO joint-defense
obligations. The European Community, collectively, and countries
such as Germany have promised financial and related assistance,
both for the front-line states (Turkey, Jordan, and Egypt) and for
the U.S. military operation; but disbursement has been slow.

Yet, Britain again excepted, there is a distinct European viewpoint. The Europeans are less willing to go to war and more willing
to seek a negotiated or compromise solution than is the Bush administration. That viewpoint has been shown by the separate foreign
policy initiatives pursued by EC foreign ministers, by the call for

33

separate European-Iraqi talks made by German foreign minister Hans-Dietrich Genscher and others, and by the recent visit of senior French envoys to Baghdad.

Even so, the differences should not be exaggerated. The January 4 statement by the EC foreign ministers was carefully worded to avoid any open split with the U.S. position of insisting upon Iraq's complete, unconditional, and immediate withdrawal from Kuwait. The agreement on a Geneva meeting between Secretary of State James Baker and Iraqi foreign minister Tariq Aziz strengthened the hand of Britain and the Netherlands in arguing against any independent EC initiative, which would be seen as weakening the unity of the anti-Iraqi coalition.

But if the Baker-Aziz talks fail, there will be fresh calls for a new European initiative, for direct talks with Baghdad, and for fresh discussions by the UN Security Council (the latter of which has been rejected by the United States).

France, Germany, Italy, and Spain, in particular, have been keen to find some face-saving formula. The EC statement highlighted what the United States has said in passing—that should Iraq comply with the UN resolutions it "should receive the assurance that it would not be subject to a military intervention." The implication is that most European countries would accept Iraq's promise to withdraw from Kuwait as sufficient reason to avoid military action.

Moreover, in accordance with its decade-old policy of favoring a Middle East peace conference, the European Community has pressed for early discussion of other problems in the region once Iraq leaves Kuwait and, according to the January 4 statement, for the establishment of "a situation of security, stability and development there." The French have gone further in offering "understandings" about such a peace conference, which Mr. Baker has ruled out as smacking too much of "linkage."

Overall, there is now a degree of mistrust over the crisis between the United States and France and, to some extent, Germany. Certainly, Genscher's initiatives have meant he is no longer quite the State Department's favorite foreign minister, as he was this time last year.

Various reasons exist for those differences, some related to geography. The European Community has a sense of closeness to Middle Eastern problems that is largely absent in the United States.

Baghdad is, after all, nearer most European capitals than Los Angeles is to Washington. The threat of terrorism is also much more direct in Europe than in the United States. American troops, property, and, of course, aircraft have been attacked by terrorists, but those attacks have occurred mainly in the Middle East or Europe. Americans would express a massive outcry, even hysteria, if there were bomb explosions in, say, Washington of the kind often experienced in London during the last few years as a result of Irish Republican Army outrages.

Both France and Italy have large Arab populations and are worried about any threat to the stability of the Middle East, which would soon affect Europe. Italy is worried that "moderate" Arab states on the other side of the Mediterranean, such as Morocco, Tunisia, let alone Egypt, could be destabilized and follow Libya's path.

France previously had close relations with Iraq—supplying large quantities of arms—and is eager to ensure good relations with the Arab world by seeking to be a peacemaker and not too closely tied to the United States. France has sought to be an independent voice within the alliance. President Mitterrand said last week that he was "a loyal friend" of the United States and respected Mr. Bush, "but I do not feel I am in the position of a second-class soldier who must obey his commanding general."

Germany, at present, is constitutionally barred from sending troops to Saudi Arabia, though it has sent planes to Turkey. Moreover, and perhaps understandably, Germany is focusing on the problems of reunification and the economic and political upheavals to the east, not least in the Soviet Union. The German public, reluctant to be involved in any military venture, appears relatively uninterested in the gulf crisis.

Indeed, many in Europe do not share President Bush's sense of the importance of the crisis. They do not believe that the Iraqi invasion of Kuwait—while it should be condemned and resisted—poses such a grave threat to world peace and to the security of oil supplies. Comparisons between Saddam Hussein and Hitler are regarded as fanciful and exaggerated. A common European view is that after the experiences of the 1980s the oil market will ensure continued supplies at reasonable prices—and anyway, the United States has been living in a fool's paradise of gas guzzling and wasteful use of energy for too long.

Britain is the interesting exception. Throughout the crisis, British views and military commitment have closely matched those of the United States. The uncompromising language used first by Margaret Thatcher and, since the end of November, by John Major has echoed the words of President Bush. Mrs. Thatcher's importance should not be exaggerated, as it tends to be by some in Washington as well as in London. While her instincts were to resist Iraqi aggression—and she helped to reinforce President Bush's strong stand when she saw him in Aspen on August 2 and 3—her position was shared by other ministers, including her successor, and reflects long-standing British interests.

To go back to Mr. Zoellick's question, Britain has always taken an international rather than an insular view of its role. That is in part a legacy of empire and, in this case, a long-standing commitment in the gulf (after all, there were more British than American hostages in Iraq and Kuwait). Britain has a continuing global vision—a recognition that national interests must be seen in a perspective that is wider than that of just Europe—even if it no longer has a global capacity.

In crises, Britain instinctively backs and identifies with the United States. There are dangers here of sentimentalizing the so-called special relationship between the United States and Britain. While a relationship undoubtedly exists in defense and intelligence matters, exaggerating it undermines Britain's growing involvement in closer European political cooperation.

Even a strong pro-European like British foreign secretary Douglas Hurd has said that because Britain was able to act independently, it was able to take the lead in Europe by announcing early its military commitment in support of the United States. That announcement, he argued, would not have happened if the United Kingdom had been locked into a common European foreign and defense policy. Yet without the process of European political cooperation to tie countries together, the alliance might have been more disunited and there might have been more free-lance diplomatic initiatives.

Looked at another way, the crisis shows how many European countries, Britain notwithstanding, see their interests as being increasingly apart from those of the United States. The end of the cold war has loosened the 45-year-old links that bound the United

States and its European allies together, and nothing has been put in their place. There has been much grand talk of seeking a new transatlantic relationship, of developing a new political role for NATO and closer U.S.-EC ties—a kind of substructure of President Bush's "new world order." But at present, the talk is little more than empty rhetoric. In part, that is because Germany has been looking inward and eastward, while much of Europe has been concerned with the problems of the 1992 single market, economic and monetary union, and eventual political unification in some federal structure. The presence of Uncle Sam seems redundant now that the bear is no longer growling across the Elbe.

The gulf crisis is also partly to blame for the lack of thinking about U.S.-European relations. My hunch is that if President Bush had devoted a tenth of the time to the Uruguay Round of multilateral trade talks that he has to the gulf crisis since August, the breakdown in the GATT talks in Brussels in December might have been avoided, since there would have been high-level political input to direct the negotiators. Another less important casualty of Washington's concentration on the crisis is that a much trumpeted joint U.S.-EC declaration of principles was launched as if it were intended to be forgotten instantly.

U.S.-European relations and the solution of some of the attendant problems, such as the future of NATO and the Uruguay Round, could be made more difficult if a war breaks out. There are obvious dangers: a distancing by some, and possibly several, European countries from the U.S.-led military action; an understandable feeling in the United States that mainly American (as well as British and some Arab) blood is being spilt to safeguard oil for Europe and the Middle East; and consequently, an isolationist reaction within the United States if the operation is seen as too costly in lives and money.

As an Atlanticist and a European, I regret that many in Europe do not realize that President Bush is the most internationalist U.S. leader they are likely to get and that they should welcome his proposals for a new partnership. Part of the problem is that he has failed to explain to Europeans, let alone Americans, what he means by his new world order.

PART II

A WAR FOR OIL?

5. The Myth of Saddam's Oil Stranglehold

David R. Henderson

Saddam Hussein has no qualms about torturing or even murdering innocent people. But many Americans believe that if he extends his control to a large part of the Arab world, he could severely damage the oil-dependent U.S. economy. President Bush has stated that if Saddam gets greater control of oil reserves in the Middle East, he can threaten "our jobs" and "our way of life."[1] Secretary of State James A. Baker III claimed in September that Saddam "could strangle the global economic order, determining by fiat whether we all enter a recession, or even the darkness of a depression."[2] On November 13, Baker stated: "To bring it down [Thank you, Mr. Secretary] to the average American citizen, let me say that means jobs. If you want to sum it [the justification for intervening in the Middle East] up in one word, it's jobs."[3]

But can Saddam impose large costs on our economy? Economic analysis of the oil market answers with a resounding no. The annual cost to the U.S. economy of our government's doing nothing in the gulf would be at most about one-half of 1 percent of our gross national product. The vaunted "oil weapon" is a dud.

One thing Saddam cannot do single-handedly is cause shortages and gasoline lines. Only the U.S. government can do that. As long as our government avoids imposing price controls, any cutback in supplies that Saddam causes will simply translate into higher prices, not shortages. That is the lesson learned from the 1970s. Countries like the United States that imposed price controls caused Soviet-style line-ups for gasoline.[4] Countries like West Germany that avoided price controls made it through the 1970s with no gas lines.[5]

That's no surprise. If governments let oil prices rise, people eliminate marginal uses but continue to use oil where it is most valuable. They take fewer shopping trips and fewer driving vacations but continue to drive to work. Utilities switch from oil to natural gas when oil becomes too expensive.[6] People insulate their houses and close off unused rooms. In a thousand different ways, oil users make subtle adjustments that—voilà—cause the amount they consume to just equal the amount supplied. The market works.

Of course, Saddam does not have to create gasoline lines to hurt the United States. Increases in the price of oil, even without shortages, hurt our economy. But they hurt less than most people think.

Take the worst-case scenario that has any plausibility whatsoever. Assume that Iraq keeps Kuwait and grabs Saudi Arabia and the United Arab Emirates. Iraq would then control virtually all Middle Eastern production except for Iran's.

The Middle Eastern oil fields were producing about 12.3 million barrels per day (mmbd) before the price run-up in late July. And they will go on producing something. However evil Saddam's actions are, he is not stupid. He does not want to grab the oil fields only to leave them idle. He wants them so that he can sell their oil.

If Saddam sold the same 12.3 mmbd as were being sold before the invasion of Kuwait, the effect of his actions on the world price of oil would be zero. Oil would sell for the precrisis price of about $20 per barrel.

Saddam probably would keep the price of oil at $20. Why? Because if he took over Saudi Arabia and the United Arab Emirates, Iraq would replace the Saudis as the dominant member of the OPEC cartel. Saddam's long-run interest, like that of the Saudis, is to sell enough oil so that we oil consumers do not make irreversible investments in substitutes for oil. According to energy economists Arlon R. Tussing and Samuel A. Van Vactor, at oil prices greater than $20 per barrel, substitutes for oil become economically feasible.[7] Natural gas is a particularly good substitute. According to the *Oil and Gas Journal*, reserves of natural gas outside the United States and Canada were equivalent to 80 years of production by the end of 1989. Throughout the 1980s, additions to natural gas reserves were three times greater than annual production.[8] In short, natural gas is a good substitute for oil, is already used in most cases where oil is used, and is in abundant supply. Those facts are presumably what prevented the OPEC cartel from raising the price of oil above $20 per barrel, except for short periods of time. If Saddam runs the

42

cartel, none of the facts change. He will not set the price much above $20, or he will suffer as a consequence.

Still, assume that Saddam would cut output to drive up the price of oil. Saddam is operating in a market where world output is about 60 mmbd. A reasonable estimate, therefore, is that he would use his newly acquired monopoly power to cut output from 12.3 mmbd to a minimum of 8.3 mmbd. That amounts to a 6.7 percent cut in world output. Granted, in the short run the demand for oil is fairly inelastic. By that I mean that small cuts in production can cause large increases in world prices. Using the Department of Energy's estimate that short-run elasticity of demand for oil is about -0.15, a 6.7 percent cut in world production would cause about a 50 percent increase in price.[9] Starting from the precrisis price of $20 per barrel, we can conclude that in the most pessimistic case plausible, the price of oil would rise to about $30 per barrel.

How much would such a price increase cost the United States? Before the crisis, we imported about 8 mmbd. A price increase would lead us to cut our imports as well as our consumption and to increase our production. But assume pessimistically—and contrary to common sense and evidence—that we would continue to import the same 8 mmbd. The daily cost of those imports would then rise by $80 million. That amounts to $29.2 billion per year.

Twenty-nine billion dollars is not small change. But put that number into perspective. It is only about one-half of 1 percent of our $5.4 trillion GNP. A loss of half of 1 percent of GNP is surely not what James Baker had in mind when he asserted that Saddam could "strangle" the world economy. Indeed, $29 billion is not much higher than economist Paul Portney's estimate of the annual net cost that the Clean Air Act will impose on the American economy.[10] And Bush and Congress, not Saddam, imposed the Clean Air Act on us. The increase in the price of oil would cost only about $112 per year per American. At the gasoline pump, the cost would show up as an added 24 cents per gallon. And that's on top of the old price of about $1.09 per gallon, for a total of about $1.33, which is about what we pay now.

Consider, by contrast, the costs of war. Sending troops to the gulf has not been cheap. The Pentagon estimates, so far, that the cost of sending the extra troops to the gulf and keeping them there will be about $25 billion annually.[11] That's on top of our regular spending to protect the gulf, Southwest Asia, and Northwest Africa, which one expert has estimated at $46 billion in fiscal year 1990.[12] And our military costs get much higher, in money and lives, if shooting starts.

Remember also that the added military spending does not guarantee success. All it guarantees is that we can keep our presence in the gulf.

Moreover, the main reason oil prices are high is the threat of war. The price of oil on the spot market has increased or decreased with the chances of war. That makes sense. Oil is difficult to produce when shots are being fired all around. Note the irony. Bush threatens war because he is afraid that Saddam will increase the price of oil. But the very threat of war, something that Bush has control over, is what increases the price of oil.

The bottom line: whatever other justifications there may be for war with Iraq, cheap oil is not one of them.

A Postscript

The preceding economic analysis may seem controversial. It is not. Well-known economists across the ideological spectrum agree with it. According to a recent article in the *San Francisco Chronicle*, free marketer Milton Friedman and liberal James Tobin, both Nobel Prize winners, agreed with the analysis.[13]

Tobin stated: "There are other ways of coping with $30- or $40-a-barrel oil than going to war. The ultimate loss to a $5,500 billion economy is less than 1 percent. It's hard to say we should go to war to save 1 percent of GNP." Said Friedman: "Henderson's analysis is correct. There is no justification for intervention on grounds of oil." Friedman stated further that Saddam's revenue-maximizing price "would be higher than a competitive price, but not that much higher, and certainly not enough to justify what we are doing in the Middle East."

Notes

[1]George Bush, "Against Aggression in the Persian Gulf," *Current Policy*, no. 1293 (Washington: U.S. State Department, August 15, 1990).

[2]Quoted in Gerald F. Seib and Robert S. Greenberger, "Bush Wants U.S. to Forgive Egypt Debt; Prolonged Presence in Gulf Is Indicated," *Wall Street Journal*, September 5, 1990, p. A3.

[3]"Tough Duty," *The New Republic*, December 10, 1990.

44

[4]See Joseph P. Kalt, *The Economics and Politics of Oil Price Regulation* (Cambridge, Mass.: MIT Press, 1981).

[5]George Horwich, Testimony on the Emergency Preparedness Act of 1981 before the Subcommittee on Energy and Agricultural Taxation of the Senate Committee on Finance, 97th Cong., 1st sess., December 8, 1981.

[6]In 1973, the last year of low oil prices, utilities in the United States used 3.515 quadrillion Btu's of oil. By 1983 they had reduced their use of oil to 1.544 quadrillion Btu's, a reduction of 56 percent. See U.S. Department of Energy, Energy Information Administration, *Monthly Energy Review*, July 1984, p. 29.

[7]See Arlon R. Tussing and Samuel A. Van Vactor, "Perspective on World Energy Markets: Real Costs Will Continue to Fall," *OPEC Review*, forthcoming.

[8]Ibid.

[9]Actually, the Department of Energy reported that the United States and Europe had an elasticity of demand of -0.15, that Canada's and Japan's elasticities were -0.12, and that other countries' elasticities were -0.17. I weighted each country's elasticity by its consumption to get the world elasticity of demand of -0.15. See David R. Henderson, "The IEA Oil-Sharing Plan: Who Shares with Whom?" *Energy Journal* 8, no. 4 (1987): 23–32.

[10]Portney estimates that the annual cost of the Clean Air Act will be $29 billion to $36 billion and that the annual benefit is likely to be about $14 billion, for a net cost of $15 billion to $22 billion. See Paul Portney, "Economics and the Clean Air Act," *Journal of Economic Perspectives* 4, no. 4 (Fall 1990): 173–81.

[11]See Andy Pasztor, "Bush Move to Boost Firepower in Gulf May Push Yearly Cost to Over $25 Billion," *Wall Street Journal*, December 3, 1990, p. A16.

[12]See Earl C. Ravenal, "Disengagement from Europe: The Framing of an Argument," in *NATO at 40: Confronting a Changing World*, ed. Ted Galen Carpenter (Lexington, Mass.: Lexington Books, 1990), p. 235.

[13]Jonathan Marshall, "Economists Say Iraq's Threat to U.S. Oil Supply Is Exaggerated," *San Francisco Chronicle*, October 29, 1990.

6. How Oil Markets Respond to Supply Disruptions

Michael E. Canes

The events of August 1990 in the Middle East were preceded by several months of bickering among members of OPEC and an agreement reached among them in July to restrain collective output sufficiently to achieve a $21-per-barrel "target" price. In the several weeks preceding Iraq's invasion of Kuwait, the world price of crude oil already had risen from about $15.50 per barrel to about $20 per barrel. However, very little of that increase had yet shown up in U.S. gasoline prices, the single most important barometer of public and, therefore, political reaction. The price behavior in the weeks preceding the invasion provides some perspective on the commonly held view that pump prices tend to rise instantaneously when crude costs rise but are slow to descend when crude prices fall.

How did markets respond to the invasion and the ensuing embargo of Iraqi and Kuwaiti oil? At the time, the embargo meant the loss of close to 4.5 million barrels per day of supply, or between 7 and 8 percent of total world supplies. The ability and willingness of others to increase output were as yet untested, including the willingness of Western governments to release strategic stockpiles. Further, some sophisticated refining capacity was lost through the embargo of Kuwait, while demand for jet fuel was buttressed by increased military use.

All of that resulted in substantially higher crude oil and oil product prices, both in the United States and elsewhere. The price of crude reflected both the reduced supply that resulted from the embargo and forward-looking assessments of what might happen should war break out between Iraq and the forces opposing it. Aggressive statements by Western and Iraqi leaders probably were responsible for moving the price past $40 per barrel in mid-October, but increased daily supplies and reassessments of possible war damage have since brought the price down below $30 per barrel.

Generally speaking, product prices rose along with crude prices, with two important exceptions. The price of gasoline rose much less in the United States than did the price of crude, even though elsewhere, in Europe and Japan, gasoline prices rose as much as or more than crude prices. At the same time, jet fuel prices rose more than crude prices did, especially in the Far East but also in the United States.

Supply-and-demand reactions to those price signals have been consistent with what economic analysis would predict. World crude supplies have increased steadily and now are enhanced by as much as or more than the amount lost through the embargo. Saudi Arabia and the United Arab Emirates account for about two-thirds of the increase, with other OPEC and non-OPEC countries each supplying about half of the other one-third. Even in the United States, where crude production has been dropping rapidly for several years, there has been a small net increase in production since August. That increase has slowed the year-to-year decline to about 1.5 percent from its previous rate of more than 5 percent.

Demand for product in the United States dropped at an average rate of 3.5 percent in October, November, and early December; worldwide demand is estimated to be at least a million barrels per day less than previously projected. How much of the lower demand is due to price-induced conservation or fuel substitution and how much to reduced economic activity is difficult to say because the activity data for the fourth quarter are not in yet. However, previous experience indicates that price changes alone may account for a good portion of the decline in U.S. demand.

In response to the increased demand for jet fuel, U.S. and other refiners have substantially increased output. The U.S. refining industry produced record monthly amounts of jet fuel in September and October and near-record amounts in November. In recent weeks, jet fuel prices have fallen substantially and now are about where they were relative to other fuel prices before the invasion.

Accurate data on worldwide petroleum inventories are difficult to come by, but U.S. numbers are up to date. Primary U.S. inventories rose slightly in the first weeks after the invasion, and judging from the pattern of product deliveries in those weeks, inventories at the secondary or wholesale level also rose. Despite criticism of that behavior in some quarters, such an increase in precautionary demand in the face of a known reduction in future supply (as tanker shipments from Kuwait and Iraq stopped) and possible further disruption in the event of war meant that more supply would be available in the future.

Beginning in September, oil futures markets began reflecting expectations that prices would fall, perhaps steeply, as supplies from new sources hit the market, and so inventories began to decline. The rate of drawdown in the United States was close to 1 million barrels per day in October and November—above normal for that time of year but consistent with market signals and a significant supply-source disruption during a period of reduced production relative to the preinvasion situation.

A number of observations can be made about all those phenomena. First and most important, the ability of market participants to act according to mainly economic and not political constraints has made a significant difference. Instead of physical shortages and gasoline lines, as experienced in the United States in the 1970s, we have simply had a rise in price followed by a decline. And instead of lobbyists' seeking ways to use price and allocation regulations to further corporate purposes, we have had operations people adjusting to changed market circumstances. Overall, that has probably saved us untold hundreds of millions of dollars in avoided waste and resulted in lower prices to consumers to boot.

What of the charge that U.S. oil companies took advantage of the situation to price "gouge"? A number of points are worth making. First, U.S. gasoline prices rose much more slowly than crude prices and, at one point, lagged by 30 cents per gallon. That helps to explain why large oil companies' third-quarter earnings were flat, while declines in refining-marketing earnings more or less matched production gains. Second, U.S. gasoline prices rose much less than European or Japanese prices did. Some ascribe that to the president's call for restraint, but it is clear from the behavior of gasoline and crude prices before the invasion that raising gasoline prices in a declining market is difficult at best. Third, there is no evidence from any quarter that publicly owned oil companies raised prices any less than private companies did. Petro-Canada, for example, moved its prices about in line with private Canadian companies and came under the same criticism for doing so. Thus, charges of price gouging, which politicians take very seriously and which form the intellectual basis for proposed price control legislation, seem to have little substance.

What is the outlook for the future? Speaking only of possible market response, in the short run, everything depends on the outcome in the Middle East and how that outcome is achieved. An outbreak of hostilities almost certainly would mean some destruction of oil producing, refining, or export-associated capital such as pipelines and terminals. How much destruction is subject to conjecture, but it certainly seems likely that Kuwaiti and possibly Iraqi oil-associated capital will be damaged, perhaps very badly. Obviously, spot and futures market participants will take account of that development if it comes to pass.

A peaceful resolution depends upon the terms. Does peace in the near term mean the end of the oil embargo or merely an agreement not to initiate hostilities? And what will be Iraq's position vis-à-vis the Saudis and others in the event of a negotiated solution? Will Iraq simply impose its will if U.S. forces are no longer a factor, or will other gulf countries generally be free to choose their oil output policies? In the long term, nongulf output and demand will adjust to any of those possibilities, but in the short term, they easily could mean a difference of $5 to $10 per barrel in the world price of crude oil.

As for public policy, the signs are mixed at best. Polling data indicate vast public anger at the oil industry, with a majority favoring almost any retribution short of outright nationalization. Political entrepreneurs at both the state and federal level are, of course, not oblivious to that sentiment, and the industry's defensive platoon is likely to be on the field a lot of the time in 1991.

The one new federal initiative of the past year, government-owned product stocks to be tried for three years on an experimental basis, is not a good idea. The initiative was undertaken to deal with events like the *Valdez*-associated gasoline price increase of 1989 or the heating oil price increase induced by the winter cold of 1989–90. However, public stocks will be expensive to maintain and manage. Also, creation of publicly owned product stocks may reduce incentives to hold private stocks. And perhaps worst of all, it is possible that public stocks won't be of much use even if the events they are supposed to hedge against come to pass. Last year's cold-weather heating oil problem, for example, was in large part a matter of delivery logistics, rather than a shortage of product. Should similar circumstances arise, political frustration conceivably could lead to commandeering of privately owned logistical resources, thereby worsening, rather than aiding, the delivery of product.

There is, however, at least one bright note. While the oil industry came in for its share of press criticism in August and September, other articles and editorials pointed out that markets were adjusting much more smoothly than they did in the 1970s under government price and allocation controls. Such press commentary is socially valuable, for it forces politicians to defend proposals to reinstitute controls instead of forcing the industry to defend its position that controls should not be imposed, as it did in the 1970s. Thus, for the moment, the intellectual case against controls prevails. Whether that case can be extended to more positive initiatives, such as opening government-owned lands to oil and gas exploration and production, remains to be seen.

7. Oil, War, and the Economy

William A. Niskanen

Oil, jobs, and the American way of life, according to the administration, are only part of what is at stake in the Middle East. My primary task is to analyze the economic effects of alternative outcomes of the gulf confrontation. That should permit all of us to focus better on the more relevant, but necessarily more nebulous, interests at stake.

The first important lesson is that the Iraqi invasion of Kuwait did not, by itself, cause the recent spike in the price of oil. The invasion, however deplorable, neither reduced the world supply of oil nor increased the world demand for oil. The recent spike in the price of oil was a consequence of the U.S. response to the Iraqi invasion, specifically the effects of the U.S.-organized embargo on oil exports from Iraq and Kuwait and the temporary increase in inventories in anticipation of a possible war. The embargo, which reduced the world supply of oil by nearly 4 million barrels a day, should have been expected to increase the price of oil to about $36 a barrel in the short run and about $21 a barrel in the long run, both relative to the price of about $18 a barrel before the Iraqi invasion. The peak price of about $41 a barrel was clearly due to the combination of the embargo and temporary inventory building in anticipation of a possible war. The unusual spread between the spot and the future prices of oil has been consistent with this perspective.

The second lesson is that the economic effects of a reduced oil supply from any region depend on a nation's net exports or imports of oil but not on the source of the imports. Specifically, the cost to the United States of an increase in oil prices is a consequence of oil imports being nearly half of U.S. consumption, even though we import relatively little from the gulf nations. As a rule of thumb, an increase in the annual average price of oil of $10 a barrel now increases the costs to U.S. consumers by about 1 percent of the gross national product and reduces real GNP by about one-half of

1 percent. Similarly, for other nations, the effect of an oil price increase on consumers is proportional to consumption, and the effect on real GNP is proportional to net exports or imports. The U.S.-organized embargo of oil exports from Iraq and Kuwait has increased the costs to consumers around the world, increased the returns to producers of oil and other sources of energy in all nations, sharply reduced the real GNP of Iraq and Kuwait, somewhat reduced the real GNP of the United States and the other oil-importing nations, and increased the real GNP of the oil-exporting nations—most substantially the gulf nations we are now defending—by about twice the net cost to the United States.

The third lesson is that an unchallenged threat of an Iraqi invasion of Saudi Arabia would probably have *reduced* the near-term price of oil. Such a threat would have reduced the security of Saudi property rights in oil, relative to Saudi-owned assets in other nations, and would probably have increased Saudi oil production and exports. The Iraqis may or may not have planned a subsequent invasion of Saudi Arabia, but their invasion of Kuwait clearly increased the credibility of that threat. The irony of the U.S. response to the Iraqi invasion is that it foreclosed the short-term economic benefits from the increased credibility of an invasion of Saudi Arabia.

The fourth lesson, based on the calculations by David Henderson, is that Iraqi control of all the oil production in the gulf, except that of Iran, would probably have only a small effect on the price of oil. As of July 1990, Iraq and Kuwait produced about 7 percent of the world oil supply (outside the communist countries). Iraqi control, either by occupation or intimidation, of the oil production of Saudi Arabia and the several gulf emirates would increase their share of current production to nearly 20 percent. The U.S. Department of Justice approves mergers of that magnitude every year. The price of oil that would maximize net revenues to Iraq, given that limited degree of monopoly power, is probably around $25 a barrel—higher than the price in July but lower than the current spot price. Such estimates are necessarily subject to some error, but there is no basis for an estimate that Iraq could maintain an oil price higher than $30 a barrel.

In summary, if we consider only the economics of oil, the costs of the U.S. response to the Iraqi invasion are higher than any potential benefits from deterring any further Iraqi aggression. Oil is clearly not worth a war.

Let's now turn to the economic effects of war. In the short run, wars have been good for the American economy. One might hope that this is not why the business community has been extraordinarily quiet about the gulf confrontation. My own estimate is that real U.S. GNP increased about 1.4 times the increase in real defense spending during the Korean and Vietnam wars. The major offsetting condition in a gulf war would be the probable increase in the price of oil caused by damage to oil loading and transportation facilities. Some representative calculations indicate the relative magnitudes of those two effects. An intense short war that increased U.S. defense spending this year by $50 billion would increase U.S. GNP by around $70 billion. A war that increased average annual oil prices by $10 a barrel (much higher for a brief period) would reduce U.S. GNP by nearly $30 billion. The net effect of the two conditions would be an increase in GNP of about $40 billion. You can make your own estimate from other war scenarios that involve different combinations of the two conditions, but there does not appear to be a plausible scenario that would have adverse short-term net economic effects on the United States. Such effects do not justify a war, but they are not an argument against a war that is important on other grounds.

The long-term economic effects of a war, however, are clearly adverse. That is why the financial markets, which pull forward or capitalize expected future effects, are so spooked by the prospect of war. Wars generally increase taxes, regulation, inflation, and the economic powers of the government. Although total government spending does not appear to be subject to any "ratchet effect" of the spending for war, many of the emergency powers authorized during a war tend to stay in place. For example, Richard Nixon's authority to impose price and wage controls in 1971 was based on emergency powers authorized in 1917. Those of us who are especially concerned about the long-term growth of the government have a special reason to be cautious about wars. In the current case, the major midterm cost of a gulf war would be the continued delay of any peace dividend from our victory in the cold war.

So far, my comments are rather standard economics, and those economists who disagree with me are probably wrong. My colleagues, however, are likely to overlook two economic dimensions of the gulf confrontation. Iraqi control of most of the gulf oil would not much increase the monopoly price of oil, but it would substantially increase Iraq's power to raise the price of oil if it chose to reduce production below the rate that maximizes its net revenues. An Iraqi government with important objectives other than maximizing wealth would thus have a larger potential to harm the oil-importing nations. A second dimension that my colleagues may overlook is that we are not indifferent to the distribution of wealth in the Middle East. If another emirate, for example, had invaded Kuwait, few Americans would have noticed and fewer cared. The record of the Iraqi government, however, makes us concerned about how it might use additional wealth; that would be the case even if the United States consumed none of the resource Iraq controlled or if we were a net exporter of that resource.

In summary, the important economic dimensions of the gulf confrontation are not its economic effects on us but on the capability of an aggressive nation to pursue policies that threaten its neighbors. President Bush has acknowledged that the gulf confrontation "is not about oil. It's about naked aggression." That is at least a relevant rationale. The important issue is whether that rationale is sufficient to merit a war.

On that issue, my views may differ from those of many of my economic colleagues. The United States has not responded and cannot respond to every episode of "naked aggression," so some other criteria must be brought to bear to identify those aggressions to which we should respond. In this case, however, the characteristics of both the aggressor and its victim do not meet the traditional criteria for a U.S. military response. True, Iraq is an aggressive nation and its leader is a vicious tyrant, but that was also the case when the U.S. government supported Iraq with naval forces in 1987 and loans in 1988, and it does not distinguish Iraq from some of our strange new allies. More important, Iraq did not harm the United States, is not a threat to us, does not have the potential to be a significant threat, and is not an agent of a larger nation, specifically the Soviet Union or China, that has been a threat. Kuwait and Saudi Arabia are feudal monarchies, more than 6,000 miles distant, with which the United States has no security agreement or significant cultural ties. The timing of the gulf confrontation is also bad. Our foreign policy attention should be focused on the dramatic developments in Eastern Europe and the Soviet Union, rather than on a sideshow in the Middle East. In summary, the gulf confrontation does not meet the traditional criteria of responding to a direct attack on or a threat to the United States or of stopping the spread of communism, fulfilling our security agreements, defending democracy, or securing our back yard. President Bush is correct to define his foreign policy vision as "a new world order," but one wonders what it has to do with the shared concerns of the American people.

For the United States, a war against Iraq this winter would be the wrong war in the wrong place at the wrong time. Our government would make a tragic mistake in initiating that war.

8. The Nature of Saddam's Threat

Richard K. Thomas

Saddam Hussein's threat to the world is military and political, not economic. Despite a lot of loose analysis, there is no purely economic justification for opposing Saddam's takeover even of Saudi Arabia, let alone Kuwait.

Instability is endemic to the Middle East. Thus, for the foreseeable future, as in the recent past, other leaders, nations, or political events will periodically threaten or interrupt oil supplies if Saddam doesn't. And absent his own political agenda, Saddam would be about as reliable a supplier and pricer of oil for purely economic reasons as the other Arab members of OPEC are now, or probably anyone else might be, for that matter.

The range of possible destabilizing political events in the Middle East is simply so great that any other conclusion is profoundly unwise. So either Saddam is worth fighting because he's a particularly bad guy, or there is no sense opposing him at all.

Saddam is a ruthless leader, grabbing for regional and world power by force of arms. That is as certain as anything ever is in politics, given the plain evidence of his own acts. Unopposed by non-Arabs, Saddam has the guns, the money, and the will to achieve his goals. Only Turkey in the Middle East might now check him militarily, and it would take an effort beyond any possible return to Turkey. Turkey is not a direct target of Saddam's plans for Pan-Arab dominance and is strong enough to maintain its own independence no matter what. Iran, another non-Arab state, is militarily exhausted.

Saddam's goals will almost certainly create a war with Israel once he has nuclear weapons to balance the Israelis'. Saddam has made elimination of Israel an important, if not the chief, political objective. As Israel's guarantor, the United States would certainly be involved when a much more powerful "greater Iraq" turned its sights on Tel Aviv, whether that is now publicly admitted or not.

Honest persons, as the saying goes, can perhaps differ about whether Saddam must be fought. Personally, I don't see two sides at all. I believe Saddam's brutality and program of conquest totally justify U.S. and UN armed opposition, including ejecting him from Kuwait. That is a moral and political judgment only. There is no underlying supposition that a triumphant Saddam would damage the world economy by manipulating prices and withholding oil for economic gain in ways that OPEC isn't trying to do now.

Oil supplies only 20 percent of world energy. It gains its leverage from (1) being the cheapest fuel to transport, (2) being internationally more transportable than other fuels, and (3) being generally the lowest cost fuel. It is dramatically the lowest cost—and the most widely profitable—fuel when produced from the massive, easily accessible geological formations that are, unfortunately, now unique to the Arabian Gulf. That low cost gives gulf nations a lock on the marginal world energy supply in any short-run time frame.

Yet in the long run there are many substitutes for oil, including conservation. And even now the competitive market imposes great long-term restraint on the upside pricing power of any and all oil producers, including those of the gulf. Arab-OPEC, or a Saddam-ized A-OPEC, could bring world energy prices decisively lower for several decades, should it so wish. But it cannot, for more than a few destructive and counterproductive years, take prices much higher than they are now.

So even if Saddam, or for that matter some other single regime, seized control of all the Arabian peninsula's oil, it would make little economic difference. The new regime's economic, as opposed to political, management of the colossal oil resource would likely approximate the management of A-OPEC now. The regime might achieve sporadic half-success in limiting volumes, thereby obtaining somewhat higher-than-market prices for its oil without doing major damage to its markets. Saddam, as A-OPEC's Saudi managers do now, would attempt to establish the best long-term revenue-maximizing price possible within the confines of his marginally effective cartel or monopoly power.

Blind stupidity, of course, is also a possibility. A single manager, if short-term greed overcame economic logic, might willfully damage the world economy by imposing and maintaining, through progressive production cutbacks, a destructively high price for several years. Such action would cause severe dislocation and economic depression in the West, indeed throughout the world economy. But a group of producers, such as A-OPEC, might do that also. Indeed, by not quickly bringing down the politically driven price shock that followed the 1973 Yom Kippur War, and by not dropping the price after the oil shocks that followed the shah's overthrow and the Iraq-Iran war in 1979–80, A-OPEC needlessly damaged its customers and damaged its long-term markets.

So it would be against the now clearly demonstrated long-term economic interest of Saddam or any producer or group of producers to jam destructive prices into the market for economic motives alone. It would lead, once again, to massive substitution and conservation efforts that within years would further destroy the long-term economic value of gulf oil.

Indeed, in purely economic terms, it is equally plausible to imagine a more benign outcome of single-manager control of the gulf oil resource. Thus, a single manager, even Saddam Hussein, might be steadier and more successful in nudging prices and volumes toward optimal long-term outcomes than the weak and hesitant Saudi Arabian regime has been in the past. There would be no Saddam to bully Saddam into uneconomic oil price decisions as there has been a Saddam, a Nasser, or a Qaddafi to bully the Saudis.

Such economic scenarios are nearly irrelevant anyway. Conscious economic judgments have counted hardly at all since the Middle East gained dominance as marginal world energy supplier in 1970–71. The dominant price force has been periodic spasms of scarcity and glut produced by political upheaval and war. Those spasms have made oil prices swing shockingly wide around OPEC's feeble efforts at long-term price rigging. The great shocks to the Western and world economies came in 1973 (Yom Kippur War), 1979 (overthrow of the shah), 1980 (Iran-Iraq War), and 1990 (Iraq's invasion of Kuwait). Prices dropped after each earlier explosion and collapsed to $10 a barrel in 1986. Once again, they are dropping— this time, even before the Kuwait issue is resolved.

Political shocks are inevitable in the future. None of the regimes in the Arab world, including Israel, rest on the full, democratically expressed consent of all those governed. Until they do, and until the regimes settle into civil and peaceful relationships, war, revolution, and the threat of war and revolution will keep intermittent disruptions of oil supplies as the region's norm—with or without Saddam Hussein.

Oil raises the stakes in everything occurring in the gulf, but oil supplies to the West are in no way at stake. Even the existing likelihood of periodic oil shocks to the West is not increased much, if at all. The only true threat is Saddam's clear, aggressive capabilities—the military actions Saddam has already taken with the guns he already has—plus the increase in potential aggressive power that Kuwait's oil wealth would give him in the future. The conquest or intimidation of Saudi Arabia would have given him vastly more resources for aggression.

Stopping Saddam in Saudi Arabia was essential to preventing him from tripling his potential income from oil. Driving him from Kuwait halves his potential income from oil and teaches his country that war won't pay. It also helps ensure that the United States won't have to besiege Saddam indefinitely, or face him later as a more formidable foe of Israel.

Those are political, humanitarian, and military reasons for halting Saddam now. Economics doesn't count. To say that economic calculations should or do drive the current U.S.-UN intervention is the equivalent of saying that the allies fought Adolf Hitler or Benito Mussolini because they were mercantilists in control of large economies. True, they did micromanage their economies in a fascist fashion, they did distort domestic and world markets, and they did damage world efficiency and growth. But it was their guns, not their economic policies, that forced the world finally to fight. So it is with Saddam.

Geological accident is the real culprit in the world's vulnerability to current events in the Middle East. Oil is still plentiful in nature, and world reserves continue to grow faster than consumption. Seismic and other geological evidence indicates that vast amounts of oil remain undiscovered. But most of the future reserves are in the Middle East, whose share of the world's proven reserves is already climbing sharply. That share was up from 57 percent in 1985, for instance, to 66 percent in 1989.

Most important, virtually all the discontinuously cheap oil reserves are now located around the Arabian Gulf and will be located there in the future. That is the crux of the energy problem.

Most gulf oil production costs are still well below $1 a barrel, versus $10 to $25 per barrel, and higher, for new oil elsewhere. The tremendous gap in costs makes the Arabian Gulf the 800-pound gorilla of energy. No matter what else happens, the gulf producers can always lower their price below all others and still eventually sell their oil at a considerable profit.

Iraq already has 100 billion barrels of proven reserves of cheap oil. Kuwait boosts Iraq's total to 197 billion barrels. Conquering Saudi Arabia and the rest of the Arabian peninsula would push Iraq's total to 546 billion barrels, or more than half the world's 1,005 billion barrels of reserves—and four-fifths of the magically cheap gulf oil. Iran has most of the rest.[1]

Thus, the paradox of Arabian Gulf oil power is not that there are scarcities and high economic prices. The paradox is that there is too much oil, which, although its supply is politically interruptible, is too cheap for the world not to use. Everybody who produces or consumes oil elsewhere is aware of that. So unless the governments of consumer nations mandate higher cost energy as an act of sovereignty, there is no foreseeable world marginal supply of spot energy, let alone oil, of any kind.

As the Israelis joke, "Think how different things might be if Moses had encountered 'No Left Turn' signs when exiting the Sinai."

Competitive forces do not severely limit the long-run price-raising discretion of the gulf producers. So the only real questions concerning gulf oil are the central questions raised by any great power. Who controls the financial, military, and political might that this inevitable wealth bestows? And what will that person or persons do politically with that power? Will the power be wielded unaggressively by the current half-dozen gulf governments, faintly led by the richest producer and reserve holder, Saudi Arabia? (And backed by the United States?) Will it be revolutionaries not yet in power in some or all of those countries? Will it be Saddam Hussein or some other single regime with the will and power to build an outsized military might with which to attack its neighbors?

Clearly, those questions have no permanent answer. They will be continuously answered day by day, week by week, month by month, year by year, by political and military events in the Middle East.

Saddam Hussein proposed himself as the (temporary) answer last August. He did so by an act of raw aggression. He has and had already announced his intention to go to war—at least against Israel—in the future. The United States and the world decided to say, no, Saddam shall not have charge of the gulf, not by aggression, not this time. Troops sent to protect Saudi Arabia ensured that.

The United States and the world are now poised near war to ensure that Saddam will not be left in control of even Kuwait. That again is a pure political issue. Joining Kuwaiti reserves to Saddam's gives Saddam no permanent additional market power whatsoever. Iraq and Kuwait hold just 20 percent of world reserves. At the moment of Saddam's invasion, Iraq and Kuwait had a far smaller share of world production (9 percent).

By contrast, Saudi Arabia still holds 26 percent of reserves. With the Saudi's satellite peninsula states included, the percentage jumps to 36. And even that confers on the Saudis only the intermittent ability to influence prices, not to set them.

Given such economic calculus, ousting Saddam from Kuwait achieves only political goals. First, it makes clear to him that in no case will his program of raw military aggression and bullying be permitted to succeed. Second, by making the first point clear, the United States and the West are probably relieved of the burden of maintaining massive standing armies in the Arabian peninsula indefinitely. That would be a politically difficult, if not impossible, trick in any case. Yet it would clearly be needed to deter a Kuwait-enriched and triumphant tyrant who would merely be marking time before bullying or warring for more. With Saddam chastened and out of Kuwait, on the other hand, token military forces should suffice to contain him.

Note

[1]Data from OPEC's 1989 *Annual Statistical Bulletin*. Figures exclude Soviet and other Second World oil.

PART III

LONG-TERM PROBLEMS
IN THE MIDDLE EAST

9. Washington's Interventionist Record in the Middle East

Sheldon L. Richman

Anyone who tries to understand contemporary events in the Middle East without cognizance of the record of American intervention in that region labors under a severe disadvantage. American intervention, particularly since World War II, is the indispensable context for grasping many important events there. The links are not always direct and explicit. But however oblique some of the connections are, they exist, and we ignore them at our peril.

Unfortunately, Americans, and especially their leaders, have no patience for history. When the American hostages were seized by Iranians in 1979, President Jimmy Carter dismissed references to the U.S. record of intervention in Iran as "ancient history." That was tantamount to calling those interventions irrelevant. Knowledge of the past, however, can help us understand deplorable actions, even though it does not excuse them.

Before looking at details, it is worthwhile to back up and view the full forest. America's interest in the Middle East can of course be summed up in one short word: oil (regardless of what President Bush might say on alternate Wednesdays). Oil is what made the Middle East, in the words of a State Department official in 1945, "a stupendous source of strategic power, and one of the greatest material prizes in world history."[1] The United States aspired to control that oil-rich region, however indirectly, because it was seen as the key to world leadership. U.S. policymakers always regarded war as potentially necessary to maintain control of the region: "threats to the continuous flow of oil through the Gulf would so endanger the Western and Japanese economies as to be grounds for general war."[2] The United States had its own oil, to be sure, but during World War II, it was widely believed to be running out. Thus, America would need to conserve domestic reserves while developing foreign sources. Hardly anyone believed that private enterprise could perform that feat without government assistance. As Republican senator Henry Cabot Lodge said, "History does not give us confidence that private interest alone would adequately safeguard the national interest."[3] Nor did the oil industry wish to keep the government out of the matter.

More broadly, during World War II, U.S. policymakers envisioned a postwar world in which America was architect and chief executive of a new world order. That order was to be one in which unpredictability was minimized, if not eliminated; in which change was closely controlled; in which American interests were paid their proper respect; and in which those interests were protected by an amenable world economic system—namely, state capitalism (as opposed to free-market capitalism). Those requirements necessitated certain conditions, most particularly, access to natural resources. In light of the postwar breakdown of the old colonial empires, which the United States aspired to succeed in some manner, enlightened American leaders understood that a new form of control would be necessary. Direct rule was rendered impractical by the awakening nationalism in the Middle East, as it was in Africa and the Far East. New forms of influence would have to be improvised. The obvious choice was the maintenance of friendly, even if brutal, regimes and, where necessary, the replacement of insufficiently obeisant regimes. Some of those client-regimes would be suited for extraterritorial duty—that is, helping to keep order beyond their borders. Those appointed gendarmeries would act as bulwarks against rivals to American influence. (The strategy of appointing proxies would be formalized in the Nixon Doctrine.)

While an American consensus was built around the Soviets as the most likely threat to "order" in the Middle East, in fact, indigenous forces, in the form of unruly nationalism, were feared most. As John Foster Dulles put it in 1958, the United States "must regard Arab nationalism as a flood which is running strongly. We cannot successfully oppose it, but we could put sand bags around positions we must protect—the first group being Israel and Lebanon and the second being the oil positions around the Persian Gulf."[4] In service of that goal, Dulles established the principle that neutrality was impossible. Nations were either for or against the United States.

That did not mean that the United States never found nationalism useful. The United States supported nationalists against King Farouk of Egypt in 1952–53 in order to weaken the position of Britain, still something of a rival at that point.[5] But when Gamal Abdel Nasser, who gained power in the crisis, was seen as a threat to American interests, the U.S. policymakers had no hesitation in trying to undermine him. His elimination was even contemplated. Then in 1956, the United States opposed the Israeli, French, and British assault on Nasser—the "Hitler on the Nile," according to the *New York Times* (how little things change).

I've used the term "American interests," but we should not be lulled into taking that concept too literally. American interests should be interpreted as the interests of the relatively small group that makes policy inside and outside of government, as well as its patrons in the corporate world. They make decisions to further their own good, although, because of various economic fallacies, they may believe the country's interests are also served. The important point is that their policies actually impede the mass of Americans from pursuing their own interests as they see them. The taxes, regulations, and government spending required by the small group's policies hurt most Americans, including most business people.

With regard to oil and, more generally, to energy, a free market, without intervention by the state, would have satisfied the needs of the American people and business without difficulty. Whoever controlled the oil of the Middle East would have needed to sell it. Private entrepreneurs seeking profit would have gravitated to the sources of energy that had the lowest costs and the most security. How much of our need for energy would have been satisfied by oil and how much by alternatives no one can say. But that is not important. What is important is that a noninterventionist foreign policy in the Middle East would not have meant impoverishment of the American economy. Does that mean the policymakers and their industry partners miscalculated? Not really. Although a free market in energy would have taken care of the American people, it would not have necessarily taken care of the interests who profited from the policies that were pursued by the U.S. government. We must assume that the policy elite, Standard Oil, and the other firms that sought U.S. intervention in the region knew what they were doing.

And what were they doing? In general, they were promoting repressive regimes on the condition that they maintain an order favorable to the elite group's interests. That is most clear in the cases of Iran and Israel, although—and here is the connection with the current crisis—it is also true of Saudi Arabia, Kuwait, and other Arabian Gulf states. U.S. intervention in the region has created fertile ground for demagogues and has made an easy target of any leader seen as beholden to the West. And, in the most vicious of circles, the resulting periodic crises have served to justify and sustain the policy.

In Iran, the United States came to the defense of the shah when his power was threatened by the nationalist prime minister Mohammed Mossadegh in 1953. The forces led by Mossadegh nationalized the oil industry and resented foreign interference. The United States joined an international economic boycott of Iran, then sent the CIA into the country to recruit mobs to create disturbances and drive Mossadegh from power. The U.S. government used the excuse that Mossadegh was sympathetic to communists, but knew that was not true. Mossadegh had opposed the presence of Soviet troops in his country after the war and was at odds with the Iranian Communist party. Mossadegh's actual offense was in not pledging fealty to American interests. When the shah was reinstalled, American interests gained their first concessions of Iranian oil.[6]

After 1953 the shah continued his repressive and corrupt regime with the help of the dreaded secret police, SAVAK, trained by the United States and Israel. The shah was one of our constables on the beat. As such, he was favored with billions of dollars of military equipment. When outright military aid was politically unfeasible, the U.S. government turned to indirect methods, such as a rise in the price of oil. The prime mover of skyrocketing prices in the 1970s was that loyal U.S. ally, the shah of Iran—with the support of the Nixon administration, especially Henry Kissinger. Higher oil revenues enabled the shah to buy weapons; in other words, they would be paid for by American consumers rather than American taxpayers.[7]

The Iranian revolution of 1978–79 was the predictable outcome of years of repression and corruption. And the ensuing anti-American violence was a predictable outcome of years of American patronage. (That violence includes the later taking of hostages in Lebanon.) More than two decades of support for an absolute monarch who put his American mission ahead of the liberty and dignity of his people resulted in a Muslim backlash that still wracks the Middle East. That is not to say that there would have been no Muslim extremism in Iran but for U.S. policy, only that extremists would not see America as the enemy.

Iran is only part of the story. Another part—a major part—is Israel. In a sense, American support for Israel is an anomaly. In the beginning, the oil industry and the foreign policy experts in the State Department opposed that support. They foresaw how it would alienate the Arab masses, and they must have been unsurprised in 1973 when the oil embargo was imposed. Something other than oil drove the decision to support the UN partition of Palestine and the creation of a Jewish state: domestic politics. Only later was it "discovered" that Israel could be a "strategic asset"—not only against the Soviets but also against Arab "radicalism" and in defense of "moderate"—that is, pro-American—Arab regimes. President Truman initially supported partition at the behest of American Zionists, but he had second thoughts after the November 1947 UN vote, when it was clear that partition would produce grievous violence. Those second thoughts were dispelled by Truman's advisers when the Democratic party was shaken badly at the polls in February 1948. In a special congressional election, the American Labor party candidate, Leo Isacson, defeated the Democrat, Karl Propper, in a heavily Jewish district in the Bronx. The key event of the contest was support of Isacson by Henry Wallace, who accused Truman of selling out the Jews. With New York's electoral votes at risk, Clark Clifford and other Truman aides opposed a shift in position on Palestine.

What the United States supported, and pressured other states to support, was the partition of Palestine into Jewish and Arab states. To the Jews, who constituted less than a third of the population, went 57 percent of the land, including the most arable land in Palestine. It is also important to note that Jews had purchased less than 7 percent of the land of Palestine by the end of 1947. The partition was gerrymandered so that the Jews would constitute just over 50 percent of the population. Thus, about half a million Palestinian Arabs were to have what they saw as an alien government imposed on them. Moreover, after the UN vote, the Zionist military forces and underground terrorist groups (Menachem Begin's *Irgun* and Yitzhak Shamir's Stern Gang) drove hundreds of

71

thousands of Palestinians from their homes, creating the refugee problem that is still with us today. Such tactics continued after Israel's declaration of independence and the 1948 war.[8]

The upshot is that the Arabs were not out of line in thinking they had been treated unjustly. They had been promised independence by the British after World War I but were denied it for the most part. Now something else was to stand in the way of complete self-determination. They did not understand why they should pay for the horrors inflicted by the Nazis.[9]

As a Jewish state, Israel by definition regards its Arab population as second-class citizens. For example, Arabs may not lease or buy state lands, which amount to 92 percent of Israel. Jews have access to resources and public services that are denied Israel's Arab citizens. Each Israeli carries an identity card that specifies the "nationality" of the holder: Jew or Arab. The resemblance to apartheid is striking.[10]

Arab—not just Palestinian—resentment of such treatment naturally has been directed at the United States, which was correctly seen as Israel's patron. Dean Rusk has conceded that the American role in the creation of Israel permitted the partition to be "construed as an American Plan."[11] The resentment stimulated by that perception has predictably spilled over to tangential issues.

With a single exception—President Eisenhower's opposition to Israel, Britain, and France in the Suez Crisis of 1956—the United States has steadfastly supported Israel morally and materially. It has given green lights to Israeli attacks on its neighbors and to repression of the inhabitants of the occupied territories. (The United Nations has been as vehement in opposing that occupation as it has in opposing Saddam's, so the differences in the American response raise disturbing questions.) The United States has increased military and economic aid in the wake of Israel's most egregious actions (the 1982 Lebanon invasion, for example). And it has given Israel free rein to use the aid however it likes. The U.S. position that Israel not use American aid to build Jewish settlements in the occupied territories has always been toothless.

Perhaps worst of all, the United States has helped establish the myth that Israel is hopelessly surrounded by rabidly hostile Arabs—terrorists by nature—who would delight in driving Jews into the sea. In fact, from the very beginning, the Arab nations have sought to avoid hostilities with Israel, even to the point of selling out the Palestinians.[12] Over the four decades of Israel's existence, there have been numerous offers to make peace. Israel, backed by the United States, has responded with repression in the territories and military force in neighboring states, and none of those acts, interestingly, is ever called "terrorism." Since 1976 the Arab states and the Palestine Liberation Organization have been on record supporting a two-state solution with guarantees of security for Israel. The solution was the substance of a 1976 UN Security Council resolution written by the PLO, a resolution rejected by Israel and vetoed by the United States. (The so-called overnight conversion of Yasser Arafat in 1988 is a myth.) Regardless of who is in power, the Israeli position remains: no talks with the PLO, no Palestinian state, no change in the status of the occupied territories. That is at the heart of Prime Minister Shamir's "peace plan."[13] The Israeli rejection of the PLO, as Shamir made clear in 1989, was "not because of the terroristic character of this organization, but because it desired to establish a Palestinian state."[14] The Palestinians are commanded to recognize Israel's "right to exist," while Palestinian rights are not even to be an issue. Thus, Washington's continuing support of Israel is a guarantee against progress on the most pressing problem in the Middle East.

For several decades, the United States has arrogated to itself the right to manage the Middle East. As a result, it has made America an object of hatred for millions of Arabs and Iranians. The ongoing confrontation with Iraq is only the latest episode. It is but one of the tragedies of American policy. Having allied itself so steadfastly with the forces of repression in the region, the United States cannot now become an honest broker there. Thus, nonintervention finds justification not only in principle and American revolutionary tradition but in empirical reality. It is time to replace political manipulation with an American policy of peaceful commerce with the nations of this troubled region.

Notes

[1]*Foreign Relations of the United States*, vol. 8 (Washington: Government Printing Office, 1945), p. 45.

[2]U.S. Senate Committee on Energy and Natural Resources, *Access to Oil—The United States Relationships with Saudi Arabia and Iran* (Washington: Government Printing Office, 1977).

[3] Daniel Yergin, *The Prize: The Epic Quest for Oil, Money and Power* (New York: Simon & Shuster, 1991), p. 396.

[4] Quoted in Michael B. Bishku, "The 1958 American Intervention in Lebanon: A Historical Assessment," *American-Arab Affairs*, no. 31 (Winter 1989–90): 117.

[5] Joyce Kolko and Gabriel Kolko, *The Limits of Power: The World and United States Foreign Policy, 1945–1954* (New York: Harper & Row, 1972), p. 426.

[6] See James A. Bill, *The Eagle and the Lion: The Tragedy of American-Iranian Relations* (New Haven: Yale University Press, 1988); Kermit Roosevelt, *Countercoup: The Struggle for Control of Iran* (New York: McGraw-Hill, 1979); and Jonathan Kwitny, *Endless Enemies: The Making of an Unfriendly World* (New York: Congdon & Weed, 1984).

[7] "Don't Blame the Oil Companies; Blame the State Department: How the West Was Won," *Forbes*, April 15, 1976.

[8] See Edward W. Said and Christopher Hitchens, eds., *Blaming the Victims: Spurious Scholarship and the Palestinian Question* (New York: Verso, 1988); Tom Segev, *1949: The First Israelis* (New York: Free Press, 1986); and Benny Morris, *The Birth of the Palestinian Refugee Problem, 1947–1949* (Cambridge: Cambridge University Press, 1989).

[9] See Evan M. Wilson, *Decision on Palestine: How the U.S. Came to Recognize Israel* (Stanford, Calif.: Hoover Institution Press, 1979); and John Snetsinger, *Truman, the Jewish Vote and the Creation of Israel* (Stanford, Calif.: Hoover Institution Press, 1974).

[10] See Sheldon L. Richman, " 'Who is a Jew' Matters in Israel," *Washington Report on Middle East Affairs*, March 1990, p. 10.

[11] Alfred M. Lilienthal, *What Price Israel?* (Chicago: Henry Regnery, 1953), p. 67.

[12] See Simba Flapan, *The Birth of Israel: Myths and Realities* (New York: Pantheon, 1987).

[13] See Thomas Friedman, "Shamir Faulted on Mideast Remarks," *New York Times*, October 19, 1989, in which Baker is quoted as saying, "Our goal all along has been to try to assist in the implementation of the Shamir initiative."

[14] Dan Margalit, *Ha'aretz*, November 29, 1989; quoted in Noam Chomsky, "The Intifada and the Peace Process," *Fletcher Forum* (Summer 1990): 350.

10. Factors for War and Strategies for Peace

Charles William Maynes

If the United States goes to war in the Persian Gulf in late January 1991, historians are likely to find that four considerations dominated U.S. policy: oil, order, security, and Israel. The question they will have to answer is whether those four factors, separately or together, justified a decision that put hundreds of thousands of American soldiers in harm's way. Or were there alternative approaches that U.S. policymakers ignored?

Oil

Future historians are likely to note with irony that the greatest threat to oil security in 1991 was the very war that the United States threatened to unleash. It was no accident that the price of oil rose when the risk of war seemed closer and fell when the risk receded. Because the Persian Gulf region contains more than two-thirds of the world's proven oil reserves, no one country should be allowed to dominate it. But historians, again with irony, will note that the United States secured the objective of oil security when it deployed enough force in the area to deter Iraq from invading Saudi Arabia.

Order

President Bush has stated that no cost is too high to pay for the creation of a new world order. But future historians will note that there was never any prospect that U.S. victory in a war against Iraq would lead to the creation of a new world order. The current coalition against Iraq was assembled only because the United States was willing to pay an enormous diplomatic cost—economic aid to the Soviet Union, amnesia about human rights violations in China and Ethiopia, and debt forgiveness for Egypt. Will a major country always be as willing as the United States was in this case to make sacrifices to rally the necessary votes in the UN Security Council?

In fact, the world should begin thinking of collective security from a regional rather than a global point of view. States at the regional level have the degree of national interest involved that justifies a blood sacrifice to preserve order. The role of the global community should be to build up regional organizations so that they can provide a measure of collective security at a price that is credible and bearable.

Security

Many proponents of war argue that, as with Nazi Germany, it is better to begin the fight now than later. To emphasize that point, the president has warned that Iraq one day may have nuclear weapons.

But future historians are likely to find the analogy with Nazi Germany false. Germany, after all, was the most populous nation in Europe after the Soviet Union. It was also the most advanced industrially, scientifically, and militarily. Although dependent on the outside world for some raw materials, it could manufacture virtually anything it needed to wage war.

Iraq is a country of 16 million people surrounded by countries with unfriendly governments and populations of more than 100 million. It is totally dependent on imports for the maintenance of its war machine. Oil represents 90 percent of its exports, which we can block. Much of the controversy over the effectiveness of the international sanctions overlooks one obvious point: Without exports, Iraq has no cash; without cash, it cannot import without credit; and no one wants to give Iraq credit. So sanctions will work even if some Jordanian or Iranian smugglers are willing to sell items to Iraq.

As for the nuclear threat, U.S. officials acknowledge that Iraq is still some distance from a nuclear weapons capability. The current embargo makes Iraq's efforts to gain that capability more difficult. In any case, the idea that Iraq could threaten the United States with such weapons is fanciful. The size of the U.S. arsenal guarantees that Iraq would be destroyed totally if one of its leaders ever used a nuclear device against the United States.

The current crisis has, however, revealed one harsh truth. Now that Israel has acquired nuclear weapons, it is only a matter of time before other states in the area acquire them. That is very dangerous because none of the states will have a second-strike option, which means that in a crisis they will be tempted to strike first. Israel understands the danger and for the first time has indicated that it might be willing to take part in serious arms control discussions involving its nuclear arsenal. Whatever happens in the gulf crisis, there will be an urgent need to develop a serious arms control regime for the area in the future.

It will also be necessary to take steps to limit the supply of offensive military equipment to the area, particularly to Iraq. It is Iraq's aircraft and tanks that make the country the menace of the region. The mobility of its military gives Iraq the possibility of conquering its neighbors. If it lost that mobility, even its chemical weapons would be useful primarily for deterrence of attack by others, not for offensive operations. Whatever happens in the current crisis, the United States must also press the major arms suppliers of the world to police carefully the flow of sophisticated military equipment into the gulf region.

Israel

Many of Israel's most ardent supporters in the United States are urging the president not only to wage war to free Kuwait but also to risk additional lives to destroy Iraq's war machine permanently. Israel's supporters obviously have the right to raise the issue of that state's security. But before large numbers of American servicemen and servicewomen lose their lives trying to eliminate Iraq's military capability, it is necessary to ask whether there are not other ways to protect Israel from its neighbors. It is time that the United States openly debate the desirability of a formal security pact with Israel of the sort that has protected the security of Western Europe for decades.

Preventing discussion of that option in the past has been Israel's reluctance to spell out what borders it would ask the United States to defend. But rather than lose American lives in a crusade to pacify the Arab world, it is time to face such tough questions.

Conclusion

From this analysis, the appropriate course for the United States in mid-January would be to continue the embargo, to continue to threaten the use of force at a later date, and to use the ensuing months to internationalize the effort against Iraq. The administration should work toward collective security action under a UN flag, with the United States contributing no more than 50 percent of the total effort. Saudi Arabia should be pressed to agree to impose conscription on its own population.

In addition, the United States should attempt to exploit the situation diplomatically. The United States is now making extraordinary sacrifices that primarily benefit others, yet it is asking very little in return. In the Middle East, the principal beneficiaries of U.S. policy are Israel, Kuwait, and Saudi Arabia.

Saudi Arabia and Kuwait should be pressed to declare publicly that they are finally willing to accept Israel as a sovereign state in the region. Israel should be pressed to reaffirm its commitment to UN Security Council resolution 242—the land-for-peace formula that the current Israeli government does not accept—and to cease establishing new settlements in the occupied territories, including East Jerusalem. The United States cannot accept linkage between the crisis in Kuwait and the conflict between the Israelis and the Palestinians, or Saddam Hussein will have an excuse to sit and wait. But the United States also cannot allow the Kuwaiti crisis to serve as an excuse for ignoring the Palestinian-Israeli dispute as the principal historic source of instability in the region.

Let us hope that when historians do turn to this crisis, they will be able to say that America's diplomats were as courageous as its soldiers and that the former did not fear new ideas just as the latter did not fear new challenges. The evidence to date does not suggest the final account will read that way.

11. America's Objectives in the Gulf
Gene R. La Rocque

We are faced with complex challenges in the Middle East today. The challenges involve political, economic, social, religious, and historical issues as well as a very dangerous military confrontation.

There are, in the gulf, about half a million soldiers on each side locked into a tense standoff. President Bush has made clear that he is prepared to order an attack on Iraq to end the occupation of Kuwait. He has indicated that any diplomatic talks will not be bargaining sessions but an effort to convince Iraq of our deadly earnestness. War is not inevitable, but if we stay on the course laid out by the president, it is a near certainty.

The United States faces three options: attack, retreat, or wait. Unless an intended or unintended provocation takes place, the decision to attack rests entirely with the United States. If we attack, the only known result will be the ultimate defeat and possible occupation of Iraq at great cost to the United States. We cannot now retreat without great loss of prestige. But if we wait and give the economic sanctions a real chance to bite, we may be able to avoid a frightening war.

Political conditions, more than logistical problems, are pushing for an early military resolution of the deadlock. Our huge force in Saudi Arabia and the gulf can be adequately supplied indefinitely before hostilities, although at considerable cost.

The U.S. intervention has produced peculiar financial consequences. High oil prices, sustained by the fear of a war, and increased Saudi production have bestowed a large windfall profit (as much as $180 million a day) on Saudi Arabia. The additional oil revenues are more than twice as much as the U.S. deployment costs, which the Center for Defense Information estimates to be about $74 million per day. This could become the first U.S. war in which the nations we defend make a handsome economic profit while we pay dearly.

The apparent window for military action is from December through March. Difficult weather and cultural conditions will increasingly take a toll on the fighting edge and morale of our forces the longer we wait. It will be politically unacceptable for the gulf states to host large U.S. military forces in the long term. NATO cannot be re-created in the gulf. Even NATO countries like Spain and Greece have pushed out some U.S. forces. After a bloody and destructive war, pressure will only increase for a rapid U.S. departure from Saudi Arabia.

Although the deaths of young American soldiers would be the greatest cost for the United States, there would be other far-reaching and unpredictable costs of military action.

The aftermath of war would be great instability in Iraq and continuing turmoil in the Middle East. The United States would have difficulty establishing and sustaining the kind of government it would like in Iraq. U.S. interests would be irreparably damaged by the perception that we sided, once again, with the "haves" against the "have nots." Syria and Iran would be emboldened by the elimination of Iraq as a Middle Eastern power center.

Any war that pitted the United States against an Arab nation and resulted in tens of thousands of deaths would polarize popular Arab feeling against the United States for decades to come. U.S. friendships with Islamic peoples from Marrakesh to Bangladesh would be undermined. Military action would likely weaken popular support for the unelected regimes in the gulf states. And every day the U.S. occupation troops stayed in Iraq, popular protest and resistance groups would gather momentum throughout the country. U.S. forces would continue to suffer casualties from terrorist-type attacks during the occupation.

There are no U.S. interests at stake worth the costs of a U.S. war in the Middle East. The invasion of Kuwait by Iraq presents absolutely no threat to U.S. military security. Given that the United States receives only about 5 percent of its energy needs from the entire Middle East, the invasion is hardly an economic threat. It is not clear that Saddam Hussein was interested in attacking Saudi Arabia after Kuwait, nor that he would have been able to keep oil prices high. Any U.S.-installed government in Iraq would still want higher oil prices, just as Saddam does, to deal with pressing economic development problems. Successful military action will not be able to preserve cheap oil.

More important, it is not primarily U.S. economic interests that are threatened by higher prices but those of other nations. A gulf war will not be conducted in defense of the United States but as a favor to friendly industrial nations and the minority of affluent, conservative Arabs in the gulf who now control the production, price, and distribution of petroleum. If our European and Japanese allies really feel economically or militarily threatened, why are they not willing to respond appropriately with full military action?

A war will open a Pandora's box of adverse political, economic, and cultural effects that cannot be measured now. It will not increase our regional influence in the long run. Nor will a continued U.S. occupation of Iraq and the region bring political "stability." There is little historical evidence that, in recent times, military occupation of a nation has brought stability over any significant period. Blunt military action will end the confrontation with Iraq but leave many other problems unresolved.

In conclusion, the costs of a military solution are too great, the political outcome undesirable, and the aftermath only more instability and violence in the Middle East.

By contrast, a political approach leading to a negotiated agreement offers the hope of increased stability, reduced violence, and an opportunity to use the same negotiating process to address the root causes of violence in the Middle East. However difficult and complex the task of forging a constructive resolution of the present confrontation may be, doing so is essential to avoiding a pointless war.

I strongly recommend that a period of up to one year be devoted to diplomatic action, initiated and implemented under the leadership of the United Nations (with the strong support of the United States), to achieve a negotiated settlement. The first agreement must be on the willingness of Iraq to begin to withdraw its forces from Kuwait. Any and all other issues proposed by both sides should also be considered so that we reach an equitable and enduring solution to Iraqi-Kuwaiti disputes.

All UN sanctions should remain in effect throughout negotiations in order to continue to weaken Iraq and compel Saddam Hussein to accept terms favorable to Kuwait. Ultimately, sanctions will force Saddam to leave Kuwait, assuming the nearly universal compliance attained so far continues. South Africa, the Soviet Union, China,

Nicaragua, and Vietnam have all responded in some degree to the pressure of international sanctions, even though none suffered the nearly total embargo now in place against Iraq. Today, no country can permanently withstand ostracism from the world community.

Economic sanctions will diminish Iraq's military capability every day they are in effect. They will reduce almost to zero the likelihood that Saddam will undertake other aggressive attacks on his neighbors. If, after one year, Iraq still refuses to agree to reasonable and necessary terms acceptable to the UN Security Council, the Security Council should then consider the option of military action against Iraq.

12. The Need to Keep Regional Powers in Check

Gerald F. Seib

One of the great ironies of the current Persian Gulf crisis is that, even as Bush administration analysts must contemplate what kind of military strike would be effective in driving Iraqi troops out of Kuwait, they also spend some of their time worrying about the flip side of that question: how to prevent a war from destroying or dismembering the state of Iraq. The reason? The administration realizes full well that a dismembered or crippled Iraq could produce a kind of regional instability just as dangerous in its own way as a ruthless, well-armed, unchecked Iraqi regime. Thus, the Bush administration, while pledging to use whatever power is necessary to prevail if war erupts, also is quietly hoping to calibrate its use of force to drive Iraqi troops out of Kuwait without bringing the entire country to its knees.

That only underscores the tricky task of keeping the various powers of this dangerous region in balance. For better or worse, that is precisely the task the United States and its Arab friends now face, regardless of whether the showdown with Iraq is resolved by war or diplomacy.

The strong American reaction to Iraq's invasion of Kuwait last August came in part out of a recognition that the invasion upset the fine and fragile balance of power that has contained the potentially explosive forces in the region. The region's powerhouses—Iran, Iraq, Syria, and Israel—had been coexisting in that delicate balance up until August 2, 1990. Those states, partly by design and partly by happenstance, kept each other in check, a situation that suited the interests of the United States and its moderate Arab friends. By invading Kuwait, Iraq threw that balance into serious question, a development that has led to such anomalies as a joint Syrian-American military deployment in Saudi Arabia and a formal Iranian-Iraqi peace treaty followed by the activation of Iranian military units along the Iraqi border.

Restoring some regional balance of power will be hard if there is a diplomatic solution to the Iraqi invasion of Kuwait. It will be devilishly difficult in the aftermath of a war. To understand why the task is necessary, though, one simply has to glance at a map and look at a little regional history. Iraq sits directly between Syria and Iran, two equally ambitious and dangerous regional powers. One of the most convenient aspects of regional politics over the past decade, from the American point of view, is that the enmity between Syria and Iran on the one hand and Iraq on the other hand has kept all three of those states preoccupied and prevented them from meddling in others' business even more than they have been. That, of course, is the long and the short of the explanation of the American "tilt" toward Iraq during its eight-year-long war with Iran.

Iraq has long held a key position in the balance of political power within the Arab world. It is an article of faith among Arabs that when Iraq is up, Egypt is down, and that when Egypt is up, Iraq is down. Those two traditional Arab power centers, situated in the eastern and western flanks of the Arab world, have been traditional rivals for power and influence. They developed a kind of uneasy cooperation during the Iranian-Iraqi war, when they felt a common interest in containing Iranian influence. In the aftermath of that war, though, the traditional competition between Baghdad and Cairo again was leading to a kind of uneasy rivalry, but one in which Egyptian and Iraqi power was in a kind of balance.

All that balance was lost when Iraq invaded Kuwait. The risk now is that power will remain dangerously out of balance if Iraq's invasion is left unchecked. Persian Gulf states, sooner or later, will find ways to acquiesce to Iraqi policies on oil pricing, the Arab-Israeli dispute, and ties to the West. Iran, which has no desire to see Iraq emerge as the superpower of its neighborhood, will be nervous and unhappy. Syria, lacking the strength it used to draw from its relationship with a formerly vigorous Soviet Union, will have lost the punch to serve as a counterweight to Iraq. Egypt's president Hosni Mubarak, having gambled all on a bet that friendship with the United States would allow him to withstand the enmity of Saddam Hussein, will be besieged and isolated. Jordan

84

will have to give free rein to the radical, pro-Saddam Palestinian elements it has unleashed. And the Israeli armed forces, needless to say, will be exceedingly nervous.

The problem is that a war with Iraq that becomes too messy could unleash a similarly dangerous chain of events. A weakening of Iraq would produce a commensurate strengthening of the regional positions of Iran and Syria. In the long run and in its own way, that prospect is as troubling as Iraqi hegemony in the gulf.

In fact, there is legitimate reason to worry that a war that cripples Iraq could lead to its literal or figurative dismemberment and the unique regional destabilization that outcome would bring. The cohesiveness of Iraq is a question mark because modern Iraq, thought to be situated on the spot of the ancient civilization of Mesopotamia, is actually a fairly young nation made up of a sometimes uneasy ethnic mix and occupying lands traditionally coveted by others. Turkish and Iranian regimes over the centuries have laid claim to much of what is today Iraq. Saddam himself proclaimed in a speech in 1980: "They used to take turns on Iraq. Turkey goes and Iran comes; Iran goes and Turkey comes."

In much the same way that Saddam claims that Kuwait is nothing but a product of British colonial map makers, Iraq's own borders are an artificial colonial creation. British diplomats sketched them out in the 1920s, mostly to serve the needs of the British empire at that time. Iraq was granted its independence in 1932, and Baghdad governments ever since have had to struggle to create a common identity among Iraq's diverse population of Shiite Moslems in the south, Sunni Moslems in the center, and Kurds in the north.

The Kurds have long sought their own nation, as have their ethnic cousins in adjoining parts of Turkey. A war that hobbles Iraq might inspire a new drive among Kurds to carve out their own state—a development that would alarm Turkey and Iran as much as Iraq and could ignite a violent reaction from them. Thus, a war that destroys Iraq could set off a secondary conflict involving other significant regional powers.

It is also conceivable that Iran might move in to lay claim to part of Iraq if Iraq were seriously weakened. Iran might not have a land grab in mind. But if, in the heat of war, it suspects that others, such as Turkey, are making a grab for Kurdish pieces of Iraq, Iran may feel compelled to stake its own claim to Shiite areas of Iraq. Alternately, if Shiite holy sites in southern Iraq were damaged in fighting, Iran might feel compelled to move north to defend those sites, if only in response to popular opinion at home. After all, Iranian troops during the Iranian-Iraqi war used to wear headbands declaring that they intended to drive to the Shiite holy sites in the Iraqi city of Karbala. At a minimum, a seriously weakened Iraq would be eliminated as the bulwark against Iranian expansionism that it was in the 1980s.

All those risks, of course, arise in addition to the very real danger that Iraq may attempt, in a war situation, to turn the conflict into an Arab-Israeli dispute by drawing in Israel. That probably would bring Jordan, which lies between Iraq and Israel, into the killing field of a fight between Iraq and Israel, perhaps thereby destroying the country of Jordan as we know it. The prospect of a destabilized Jordan lying to the east of Israel and the south of Syria should be enough to keep American and Israeli officials awake at night.

Therefore, neither a policy that avoids war with Iraq nor one that ensures a war to expel Iraq from Kuwait will necessarily solve the problem of restoring a regional balance that prevents an equally dangerous situation from arising in the future. Some other avenues, however, might have a greater chance of success.

One alternative would be to build a new kind of regional security structure to replace the fragile balance of power that has been disrupted. From the American perspective, the most promising development toward that end is the emergence of a new Egyptian-Saudi-Syrian axis as a result of the Iraqi invasion of Kuwait. The question is whether that axis is merely a marriage of convenience or a lasting partnership that can bring some stability to the region.

Here, as in so many developments in the Middle East, there is a wonderful irony. Those three nations have been aligned against Iraq before. But that was in the 1950s and under a total role reversal. In those days, it was Iraq that pursued a policy of cooperation with the West in security arrangements, through the British- and American-inspired Baghdad Pact. And it was Egypt, Syria, and Saudi Arabia that united in a loose coalition to oppose that dastardly Iraqi cooperation with outside forces of the West.

The bad news for the United States is that the Egyptian-Saudi-Syrian marriage of those days didn't turn out to be an enduring one. And it's hard to see how the three states, so dissimilar in so many ways, can find lasting common ground today. Egypt is a secular nation with close economic and military ties to the West. Saudi Arabia is a fundamentalist Islamic monarchy that has been openly disdainful of Egypt for most of the years since the Camp David accords. Syria is a Baathist regime, disdainful of the kind of ties to Washington that have been a staple of Egyptian policy for more than a decade, and at least philosophically disdainful of the kind of monarchy that rules Saudi Arabia. Beyond their fear and loathing of Iraq's invasion of Kuwait, it's hard to see what unites the three countries.

But at the same time, Iraq's invasion of Kuwait has thrown out all the old rules of behavior in the Middle East and made the once unthinkable now thinkable. So it's at least conceivable that the tripartite Egyptian-Saudi-Syrian axis could survive and become the foundation of some kind of regional security structure.

Another possibility is to build upon the new American-Syrian relationship and resurrect the old idea of a "comprehensive settlement" of the Arab-Israeli dispute in a way that fundamentally changes the region's politics. In recent years, American peace efforts in the region have grown narrower and narrower, finally focusing on the simple attempt to organize negotiations between a handful of Palestinians and someone in the Israeli government. The renewal of a working relationship between Damascus and Washington raises at least the chance of again thinking in the broader terms of an all-encompassing Arab-Israeli peace process— a process in which the Arab nation states participate and under which the Palestinian issue might be addressed in a broader context. Such an outcome would so radically change the power equation in the region that the old equation could be thrown out.

The only certainty is that a failure to address the balance among the regional powers could produce a situation down the road as dangerous as the powder keg the world is now watching so carefully.

13. Enduring Middle Eastern Quagmires

Leon T. Hadar

Science historian Thomas Kuhn argued that scientists tend to cling to old theories and models—paradigms—even though those paradigms cease to explain reality. Foreign policymakers and analysts also tend to sustain decaying paradigms, until major crises, especially wars, occur and cause the relevancy and costs of those paradigms to be questioned.

In a way, the initial consensus that developed in Washington about the need to assert American power against Iraq reflected such a foreign policy paradigm. That knee-jerk reaction—assuming that the United States must "do something" when anything bad happens in the Middle East—stood at the center of America's Middle Eastern paradigm during the cold war. The old paradigm suggested that without American diplomatic and military leadership, a crisis in the Middle East could produce one or more of the following scenarios: an attempt by the Soviet Union to expand its power there, a cut in the oil supply from the area, or a threat to the existence of Israel.

To put it another way, it is very doubtful that President Bush, even in this "defining moment in history," could have mobilized support for sending troops to contain, say, an invasion of Kashmir by a bloody Pakistani dictator controlling weapons of mass destruction. The reason he could mobilize support against Saddam Hussein was that Washington was conditioned by the old paradigm to expect that Middle Eastern crises, almost by definition, would harm core American national interests.

There is a need in the post-cold-war era for a new Middle Eastern paradigm. Instead, Washington is reactivating the old paradigm, which does not reflect the new realities of American interests in the area.

What are the new realities? First, the threat of Soviet expansionism and troublemaking is now largely absent from the region's equation. Moscow, however, will continue to be concerned over the possibility that chaos in its Middle Eastern back yard will spill into its Moslem republics. It will continue to demand full membership in the Arab-Israeli peace-process club, and it will continue to oppose a permanent American military presence in the area.

It is American actions and inactions—the continued support for the Shamir government's refusal to convene an international peace conference and the outbreak of a war in the gulf—that can threaten American-Soviet cooperation in the region. In the case of a prolonged and bloody war in the gulf, combined with a lack of resolution of the Palestinian-Israeli problem, Moscow would eventually have no choice but to distance itself from Washington in order to defend Soviet interests in the Arab and Moslem worlds.

Second, since 1973 there have been major changes in the political and economic dimensions of the international oil market and their impact on American interests. It might have been the responsibility of the United States, as the hegemonic power during the cold war, to pay the economic and military costs of helping the relatively weak European nations and Japan to gain access to Middle Eastern oil. There is, however, an element of the theater of the absurd in the situation today. Europe and Japan are reasserting their protectionist policies against the United States, while Washington is going to defend their economic interests as part of a costly war to which they are contributing very few resources.

Third, the long-term threats to Israel's existence do not emanate from Baghdad but are a result of the continued occupation of the West Bank and the Gaza Strip and of Israel's bankrupt economic system. Those developments and the power of the militant Shamir government are actually perpetuated by the current level of American aid to the Jewish state, which cannot be justified in the post-cold-war era on the basis that Israel is playing the role of an anti-Soviet strategic asset.

The end of the cold war, therefore, raises critical questions about the three parts of the equation that provided the basis for American involvement in the Middle East: superpower rivalry in the region, the commitment to securing the flow of oil to the West, and support for Israel.

Instead of raising questions, most policymakers and intellectuals are trying to sustain the old paradigm. The Bush administration,

90

for example, is now assuming new responsibilities in the Middle East, such as securing the power of the gulf's decaying monarchies or maintaining Israel's regional nuclear monopoly. There are also signs of new ideological crusades to sustain American intervention, ranging from the need to contain Moslem fundamentalism and Arab radicalism to the idea of making the Middle East safe for democracy.

There is no question that the end of the cold war will not bring stability to the Middle East. The area will be plagued by major upheavals in the coming decade. The struggles will involve decaying monarchies, such as Saudi Arabia; religious fundamentalism, symbolized by Iran and its supporters throughout the region; and secular military dictatorships of the benign type (Egypt) and the ruthless version (Iraq). There will be traditional, regional balance-of-power conflicts, like those between Saudi Arabia, Iraq, and Iran or between Egypt and Iraq. And there will be growing antagonism between the haves and the have nots, wars over regional resources such as water, and conflict between Zionism and Arab nationalism.

The question that should be asked is, should the United States, indeed, *can* the United States, do anything to solve such problems?

The American search for, and support of, "reformers" and "good guys" in the Middle East has little prospect of success. Indeed, American moves to contain "extremist" or to back "moderate" elements typically backfire. The Reagan administration prevented a victory by Tehran during its war with Iraq and, as a result, helped to solidify the power of Saddam Hussein. The defeat of Iraq by the United States would lead to a rise of Syria and Iran as growing threats to Saudi Arabia and Israel, threats that the United States would be asked again to contain.

Moreover, assuming that Washington gets rid of Saddam, who is going to replace him? An Iraqi Thomas Jefferson? And even if that could be achieved, who would keep that enlightened leader in power? and for how long? and with what consequences?

Some observers compare the possible long-term involvement of the United States in the gulf and the Middle East to the commitments to Western Europe and South Korea. Those commitments, however, were based on clear rules of the game, which produced certain stability in the relationship between the major cold-war players. Such rules are missing in the Middle East. There, the

United States would find itself operating in a kind of political and military kaleidoscope. Every turn of that kaleidoscope creates new and unpredictable configurations, involving a mishmash of ethnic, religious, national, regional, and international players. A foreign player like the United States who provides support for a local elite tends to create unfulfilled expectations and to become a symbol of evil in the eyes of opposition forces. For every friend the outside power wins, it is liable to gain 10 enemies.

Reality suggests that it would be impossible for Washington to neatly confine its future activity in the area to limited involvement in low- or mid-intensity conflicts, on the side of this or that player. Any "surgical" military strike develops inevitably into a full-scale operation involving all the parts of the region's body politic. Linkage is indeed the name of the game; there is no way to avoid it.

The costs of such involvement in the Middle East were tolerated by the American people during the cold war because of the perceived Soviet threat. It is unlikely that such costs, which would be highlighted during a gulf war, would be acceptable to the American people in the post-cold-war era.

What is needed is a foreign policy paradigm shift, a new Middle Eastern paradigm based on more selective involvement in the area and on a greater diplomatic and security role for Europe there. Geographic proximity, demographic ties, economic interests, and even cultural relationships all point to the need for the European powers to abandon their free-rider position and for Washington to return to them the torch of Middle Eastern leadership it inherited in 1945.

It is not enough, however, to complain about Europe's free-rider problem and call for more burden sharing. The Europeans (and the Japanese) can argue, and rightly so, that there is no taxation without representation. If the United States wants European nations to share in the costs of a security and economic engagement in the Middle East, then it should also allow them to share in the decisions affecting central regional issues—the Arab-Israeli conflict, for example.

Washington, however, wants to have its cake and eat it too. It wants to continue to dominate the policy process, yet it expects other powers—Europe, Japan, and the Soviet Union—to pay the costs of its unilateral action.

The European Community is taking upon itself new economic responsibilities in Eastern Europe. That shows that when Washington is constrained, other players who have interests in a particular area (if treated as equal players in the diplomatic game) do not hesitate to take the initiative.

The European interests in the Middle East are clear. The constraints on American involvement in the area are also obvious, and they include not only the costs of war but also the price of peace. Even assuming that the Persian Gulf crisis or the Palestinian-Israeli conflict is solved in some manner, it is unrealistic to expect a rerun of the American security and financial commitments that followed the Camp David agreements. Here, Europe and Japan can play an important role.

A united Europe can invite Israel, Jordan, and a Palestinian entity to join its community as associate members following a political settlement. If they choose, Europe and Japan can even finance a regional Marshall Plan that would include help for settling Soviet-Jewish immigrants and Palestinian refugees and support for reconstructing the economies of Iraq and Iran.

In September 1990 Italy and Spain, with the support of France, launched a plan for a Permanent Conference on Security and Cooperation in the Mediterranean (CSCM). The initial drive behind the plan is the governments' concern over the possibility that the surge of Islamic fundamentalism and deepening poverty may produce new waves of Moslem refugees to their countries.

The emphasis until now has been on social and economic issues and on ties between southern Europe and North Africa. However, the CSCM could gradually extend to other parts of the Middle East and could develop into a forum that would include the Eastern Mediterranean, the gulf region, Iran, and, ultimately, perhaps even the Balkan states and the Soviet Union. It could also cover diplomatic and security issues, such as the Arab-Israeli conflict. The United States should encourage the work of the CSCM as well as other manifestations of European initiative in the region.

PART IV

AMERICA'S UNFINISHED AGENDA

14. The Persian Gulf: Restoring the Congressional War Power

Doug Bandow

When asked about Congress's role in the Persian Gulf crisis late last year, an exasperated President Bush said that the Constitution didn't require him to consult with 535 different legislators. He's right. What the Constitution actually requires is that he abide by their decision about whether or not the United States goes to war. The president may refuse to "consult" with Congress if he wishes, but he cannot legally attack Iraq without congressional approval.

Under pressure, the president reluctantly accepted the inevitability of a congressional vote, but he clearly expected Congress to rubber stamp his decisions. Observed one aide before the vote, "The single most important thing at the end of the day is to have no language limiting the president's ability to act."[1] Moreover, the president indicated that he would ignore Congress if it attempted to limit his power. When asked if he needed legislators' assent and whether he would be bound by their decision, Bush responded, "I don't think I need it." He said that "many attorneys" had advised him that "I have the authority to fully implement the United Nations' resolutions."[2]

In short, President Bush threatened to violate the clear meaning of the Constitution and the equally unambiguous intentions of the nation's Founders if Congress refused to cede to him its power to decide on war or peace. That threat alone may have been enough to sway the three votes that would otherwise have denied Bush a majority in the Senate. Moreover, although Congress's vote to authorize the use of force in the gulf resolves the issue today, it leaves standing the president's claim that he has a unilateral right to go to war, creating the likelihood of future constitutional crises if Bush acts to implement his vision of the United States as the world's policeman.

The Historical Record

There are few issues involving the framing of the Constitution on which the historical record is clearer than it is on the issue of war powers. The American colonists lived in an age of expansive states run by strong executives wielding enormous power. The Founders of the new republic revolted against that tradition, citing "repeated injuries and usurpations" by King George in the Declaration of Independence. They also consciously avoided the European model when they created the new federal government, an approach that was evident in foreign as well as domestic affairs.

Article 1, Section 8(11), of the Constitution states that "Congress shall have the power . . . to declare war." The president was made commander in chief, but he was to fulfill his responsibilities within the legal framework established by the Constitution and subject to the control of Congress. Wrote James Madison in 1793, it is necessary to adhere to the "fundamental doctrine of the Constitution that the power to declare war is fully and exclusively vested in the legislature."[3] Although some advocates of expansive presidential power made much of the convention delegates' decision to change Congress's authority from "make" to "declare," Madison explained that this action was intended simply to give the president the legal authority to respond to a sudden attack. Observes Judge Abraham Sofaer, "Nothing in the change signifies an intent to allow the president a general authority to 'make' war in the absence of a declaration."[4] In fact, when Pierce Butler of South Carolina proposed giving the power to start war to the president, Elbridge Gerry of Massachusetts said that he "never expected to hear in a republic a motion to empower the executive to declare war."[5]

The reasoning of the conferees, who defeated Butler's motion, was simple. Explained Virginia's George Mason, the president "is not safely to be entrusted with" the power to decide on war. Mason therefore favored "clogging rather than facilitating war."[6] James Wilson, an advocate of a strong presidency, observed at the convention that the new system "will not hurry us into war." Instead, he added, "It is calculated to guard against it. It will not be in the power of a single man, or a single body of men, to involve us in such distress; for the important power of declaring war is in the legislature at large."[7] Similarly, Thomas Jefferson wrote, "We have already given . . . one effectual check to the dog of war by transferring the power of letting him loose, from the executive to the

98

legislative body, from those who are to spend to those who are to pay."[8]

Even Alexander Hamilton, much more the nationalist than Jefferson, agreed with his long-time adversary on this point. In the 69th Federalist he explained:

> The president is to be commander and chief of the Army and Navy of the United States. In this respect his authority would be nominally the same as that of the King of Great Britain, but in substance much inferior to it. It would amount to nothing more than the supreme command and direction of the land and naval forces . . . ; while that of the British King extends to the declaring of war and to the raising and regulating of fleets and armies; all of which by the Constitution would appertain of the legislature.

In short, if one takes the Constitution seriously, one can only conclude that it is Congress that must make the final decision about war and peace. That does not mean there are no gray areas, particularly regarding the president's unilateral authority to make military deployments that, while formally defensive, risk war. But despite the obfuscations offered by President Bush and his advisers, the existence of some unclear cases does not mean there are no unambiguous instances where congressional approval is required, such as an invasion of Iraq.

Does an Exception to the War Powers Clause Apply?

A number of advocates of an expansive presidential war power—oddly enough, many of whom claim to believe in a jurisprudence of "original intent" tied to the text and history of the Constitution—have advanced reasons why President Bush had the legal authority to unilaterally order an attack on Iraq. For example, Robert Turner of the Center for National Security Law claimed that the president's policy was defensive. "When the president seeks to respond defensively against Saddam Hussein's aggressive war (a crime against all nations under international law), he no more becomes the aggressor than did Franklin D. Roosevelt through the Normandy landing. The president's military pressures on Saddam are in no way an infringement on the power of Congress to veto an executive decision to launch an aggressive war."[9]

However, in opposing the Butler motion to empower the president to decide on war, Roger Sherman of Connecticut stated that "the executive should be able to repel and not to commence war."[10] Sherman (and his colleagues) didn't distinguish between aggressive and defensive wars; rather, he said the president must go to Congress to "commence war." Turner's strongest argument is that Bush's initial decision to send troops to Saudi Arabia to forestall what he viewed as an imminent invasion by Iraq—irrespective of how misguided a policy many others and I believe it to be—was "defensive" and constitutional because of the vast expansion of what some today view as the "national interest." The president's authority in this case—and his subsequent duty to gain congressional approval for maintaining the deployments after having met what he claimed to be exigent circumstances—can at least be seriously debated. But no similar claim could be made to justify the president's deciding to attack Iraq. It is Orwell-speak to call an invasion of Iraq and occupied Kuwait defensive. Indeed, no one doubted that the allied landing on D-Day was offensive; it occurred *after* Congress's declaration of war on Germany, however. It is inconceivable that Roosevelt would have claimed the legal power to invade Europe without congressional consent.

A related argument made by the Washington Legal Foundation in its amicus brief in one of the war powers cases was that a state of war existed before the administration acted. "In the case at bar, President Bush has not initiated a war and is not proposing to initiate a war. Saddam Hussein of Iraq has initiated war by invading Kuwait, seizing and detaining hundreds of American citizens and imposing a siege on the U.S. Embassy in Kuwait."[11] There is no doubt, of course, that Saddam started a war with Kuwait, but that is irrelevant to the requirements of the American Constitution governing the entry of this nation into war. The Founders empowered the president to respond to an attack on the United States, not to unilaterally intervene in wars between other states.

Moreover, while the seizure of the hostages may have been an act of war, it did not mean that the United States and Iraq were legally at war nor that Congress should not have decided on whether to start general hostilities. Individual acts of war are relatively common around the globe, and most do not lead to a state of war between nations; presidents normally respond with force proportionate to the circumstances rather than invade the offending state. In fact, President Roosevelt went to Congress for a declaration of war even after the Japanese attack on Pearl Harbor. He also did not commence full-scale hostilities against Germany, despite a small-scale shooting war in the Atlantic between German U-boats and American vessels, until after Germany had declared war on the United States and Congress had responded in kind.

Finally, it has been commonly argued that whatever the Founders may have intended, ample precedent exists for the president's deciding to go to war without a congressional declaration. Writes legal columnist L. Gordon Crovitz, "Throughout its history of some 200 deployments of troops abroad, the U.S. has had but five declared wars."[12]

However, the fact that previous presidents have acted unilaterally and unconstitutionally does not empower the current president or future ones to act lawlessly.[13] Moreover, the widely cited 200 figure is a meaningless amalgam: Many of those cases were carried out with colorable congressional authority; others resulted from military officers' acting without presidential approval; several resulted in executive punishment of those officers for their overzealousness. Some involved presidents' lying to cover up what they recognized to be violations of Congress's constitutional prerogative, and most were minor instances, offering no precedent for transporting one-fourth of the nation's military to the Middle East and invading another country. All told, conclude Francis Wormuth and Edwin Firmage: "The number of cases in which presidents have personally made the decisions, unconstitutionally, to engage in war or in acts of war probably lies between one and two dozen. And in all those cases the presidents have made false claims of authorization, either by statute or by treaty or by international law. They have not relied on their powers as commander in chief or as chief executive."[14]

Practical Objections to a Congressional Role

The fact that the Constitution requires congressional assent for the initiation of hostilities against Iraq should have been enough to compel President Bush to go to Congress. But advocates of unilateral presidential war making contend that whatever the law, the involvement of Congress is impractical today. For instance, President Bush originally said that he would welcome a vote endorsing his policies, but he warned that an adverse decision, or even a debate, would show "disunity," giving aid and comfort to Saddam Hussein. Even if it were self-evident that Bush's policy is the correct one—and it is not—dissent is the price that he has to pay for being the president of a constitutional republic that limits governmental power and guarantees free speech. The Founders intended that Congress, not the president, decide when to take the nation into war; if President Bush wanted to demonstrate national unity, he should have made his case to the public months ago and asked Congress to pass a conditional declaration of war on Iraq, instead of seeking to squelch debate.

Critics of Congress's war-making power also argue that the legislature is too cumbersome to make international policy. While it would be difficult for 535 legislators to direct the course of an attack on Iraq—which is why the Constitution made the president commander in chief—Congress's debate leading up to the vote on January 12 proved that there is no similar problem with the legislature's debating a yes or no decision on war. True, Congress has tended to shirk its responsibility in past conflicts, seeking to leave the hard decisions up to the executive branch. In the case of the Persian Gulf, legislators waited five months—after the president had painted them and the nation into a corner—to act. But a president who took the Constitution's division of powers seriously would force Congress to face up to its duty to decide by requesting legislators' consent for his proposed course of action.

Conclusion

There is no more important issue than war and peace. We can scarcely call ourselves a republic if the legislature can vote on the level of farm subsidies or tax rates, but not on whether thousands of young Americans are to be asked to die or U.S. taxpayers are forced to spend tens of billions of dollars to kill large numbers of foreign citizens.

In fact, the USSR apparently recognizes that any serious move away from totalitarianism requires limits on executive war making. In October 1989 Mikhail Gorbachev's adviser Yevgeny Primakov said that in the future "there can be no decision of that sort without the involvement of the Supreme Soviet." There would be no more Afghanistans, he promised. "There can be no repetition of the situation where a very small group of leaders take a decision that is not endorsed by the legislative authorities."[15]

President Bush should learn a lesson from Gorbachev. Although Bush won legal authority from Congress to act against Iraq, he still refuses to accept the award of war-making powers to Congress by the Constitution to which he has sworn allegiance. As a result, in the future, this or another president may again attempt to unilaterally take the nation into war to preserve feudal monarchies, keep gas cheap, save jobs, punish aggression, enforce nuclear nonproliferation, police a utopian new world order, or achieve whatever other goal registers well in the polls. But then, as now, the decision will not be his to make. Only Congress may declare war.

Notes

[1]Tom Kenworthy and Ann Devroy, "Congress Sets Debate on Authorizing Gulf War," *Washington Post*, January 8, 1991, p. A1.

[2]"President Bush: 'The Choice of Peace or War Is Really Saddam Hussein's to Make,' " *Washington Post*, January 10, 1991, p. A27.

[3]Jack Germond and Jules Witcover, "To Declare War or Not To—A Constitutional Crisis?" *San Diego Union*, December 14, 1990, p. B11.

[4]Abraham Sofaer, *War, Foreign Affairs and Constitutional Power: The Origins* (Cambridge, Mass.: Ballinger, 1976), p. 22.

[5]Leon Friedman and Burt Neuborne, "The Framers, on War Powers," *New York Times*, November 27, 1990, p. A23.

[6]Ibid.

[7]J. Elliott, comp. *Debates in the Several State Conventions on the Adoption of the Federal Constitution As Recommended by the General Convention at Philadelphia in 1787* (Cumberland, Va.: J. River Press, 1989).

[8]Francis Wormuth and Edwin Firmage, *To Chain the Dog of War: The War Power of Congress in History and Law*, 2d ed. (Chicago: University of Illinois Press, 1989) p. 299.

[9]Robert Turner, "Constitutional Controversy (cont.)," *Washington Post*, December 23, 1990, p. C5.

[10]Ibid.

[11]Daniel Popeo et al., Brief in *Michael Ray Ange v. George Bush, et al.*, December 5, 1990, p. 41 (photocopy).

[12]L. Gordon Crovitz, "War Is Too Serious to Be Left to the Judges," *Wall Street Journal*, January 2, 1991, p. A7.

[13]Wormuth and Firmage, pp. 135–42.

[14]Ibid., p. 151.

[15]Robert Pear, "War-Powers Curb on Kremlin Seen," *New York Times*, October 28, 1989, p. 6.

15. The Hijacking of Post-Cold-War American Security Interests

Rosemary Fiscarelli

For the past four decades, U.S. foreign policy has revolved around the premise that our security was threatened on a global scale by a hostile and expansionist-minded, nuclear-equipped superpower, the Soviet Union. The policy of containment was developed to meet that challenge, resulting in an enormous American military establishment with commitments around the world. The clear conclusion to be drawn from the revolutionary events of 1989, however, is that the Soviet Union can no longer be considered the political or military equal of the United States. Furthermore, the cold-war rivalry between the United States and the Soviet Union, which has colored all foreign policy considerations, appears to have finally ended. That watershed is significant because particular U.S. policy options now can be debated on their merits and not on how they relate to the superpower rivalry.

During the first half of 1990, a tremendous wave of reexamination of U.S. security concerns began, and many standing assumptions and policies were in the process of being rethought and debated on the basis of the new operating principles. The Bush administration's massive response to the Iraqi invasion of Kuwait, however, has focused the attention of policymakers and the public on developments in the gulf. Such an all-consuming redirection ill-serves fundamental American security interests. The administration's obsession with what properly should be regarded as a peripheral U.S. interest[1] has come at the expense of developing and articulating critical long-term security policies. In particular, three weighty issues central to the long-term security interests of the United States have been hijacked and relegated to the periphery by the preoccupation with the gulf: U.S. relations with Europe and NATO, the development of new policy vis-à-vis the Soviet Union, and the future of arms control.

Europe and NATO

The virtual collapse of the Warsaw Pact, the reduced Soviet threat, and the reunification of Germany have fundamentally altered the security equation in Europe. Consequently, the American role in NATO, predicated on the cold-war division of Europe, has been the subject of intense transatlantic debate. Deep cuts in the U.S. military commitment to Europe have been seriously discussed, and there has been encouraging movement toward the assumption of greater responsibility for European security by the Europeans under the auspices of the Western European Union (WEU), the European Political Community arm of the European Communities, and the Conference on Security and Cooperation in Europe. The inauguration of the conference on Security and Cooperation in the Mediterranean, a forum in which the southern European and North African states will use the Helsinki process to work on security issues of mutual concern, has been a particularly bright spot in the trend toward the development of regional security efforts in the emerging multipolar world. Recent significant changes in the governments of key European states (Germany, the United Kingdom, and France), however, underscore the variable politico-military situation in Europe. Given the predominant role of Western Europe in current American security planning and military commitments, serious attention needs to be devoted *now* to evaluating American long-term interests in that region.

During the same time, the emerging democracies of Eastern Europe have added new dimensions to European security questions. The complex process of transforming those societies into modern, liberal democracies has only begun. That transition is complicated by the rise in oil prices and by the dissolution of COMECON, one effect of which is to make trade with the Soviet Union far more costly. Meanwhile, the divisive forces of nationalism have reemerged in the trail of the retreating cold-war glacier. For example, Yugoslavia, a federation of six republics, is seething with nationalist and ethnic unrest that threatens to boil over at any time. The imminent possibility of several East European countries exploding in internecine ethnic fighting, which could drag the United States, the West Europeans, and the Soviet Union into the fray, deserves far more comprehensive and forward-looking examination than it is currently being accorded.

106

The European Community is a major trade partner of the United States, accounting for nearly one-fourth of U.S. foreign trade. That aspect of U.S.-European relations is also critical to long-term American security. The European Community is making great strides in its march toward a single economic entity; if it meets its projected 1992 deadline, it will be the largest economy in the world. Meanwhile, trade relations between the United States and the EC countries have suffered because of the failure of the Uruguay Round of the GATT talks. Given the enormous amount of trade between the United States and the European Community, and the importance of the particular nature of the trade between them, U.S. interests would have been much more effectively served had George Bush turned his vaunted diplomatic skills to the task of building an international coalition opposing trade barriers. In fact, the already-stalled GATT negotiations may be suspended indefinitely in the event of a gulf war[2]—a grave and unnecessary consequence of the obsession with the gulf.

The Soviet Union

After five years, Mikhail Gorbachev's political and economic reforms in the Soviet Union have reached a critical juncture. The difficulties of transforming a command economy into a market economy are exacerbated by the ardent nationalism of the various ethnic groups within the Soviet Union, many of which advocate independence. That struggle has recently come to a head in the debates over a new union treaty delineating the division of rights and responsibilities of the constituent republics and the all-union government. The possibility of a violent breakup of the Soviet Union is not unthinkable, and that could have serious consequences for American security. Compared with that prospect, the gulf crisis pales in significance.

Another critical facet of change in the Soviet Union is the power struggle between reformers and hard-line reactionaries. In December, Foreign Minister Eduard Shevardnadze, a key Gorbachev ally, dramatically resigned in protest against the dictatorial powers being assumed by the central government and the Soviet president in particular. There are increasing signs that the hard-liners are gaining ascendancy in the Soviet power struggle, and in the aftermath of the violent crackdown in Lithuania, there is considerable speculation about whether the middle-of-the-road Gorbachev has lost out to a disgruntled military or KGB. Given the size and sophistication of Soviet military capabilities and the threat they would pose should they come under the control of elements manifestly hostile to the United States, the Bush administration's concentration on the far more limited arsenal—in terms of numbers as well as accuracy and range—available to Saddam Hussein is a serious error in setting priorities.

Arms Control

Cold-war arms control efforts generally attempted to achieve stability by codifying the balance of terror, through imposition of reductions in military capabilities, between the superpowers. As it does in other areas, the passing of the cold war requires a critical reexamination of both the fundamental premises and institutions of arms control in order to determine its future course. The preoccupation with the gulf crisis both relegates that reassessment to the sidelines and causes neglect of three areas of vital concern to the security of the United States: START (strategic arms reduction talks/treaty), CFE (conventional forces in Europe), and weapons proliferation.

A U.S.-USSR START treaty to reduce strategic arms is vital to long-term American security. The Soviet strategic arsenal poses the most direct and potentially devastating threat to the United States. Whereas in the past the Soviets tended to be intransigent in arms control negotiations, internal problems have now made them considerably more willing to deal.[3] START thus presents a rare opportunity to lock in significant arms reductions. Unfortunately, the gulf crisis already appears to have slowed the START process: the treaty signing has been delayed until February 1991 and could be delayed even further. Given the seeming ascendancy of hard-liners in the Soviet leadership (who would probably resist decreases in Soviet military capabilities), the possibility of a breakup of the USSR itself (which could jeopardize the central government's control over strategic weapons), delays in START, which will cut strategic weapons by 30 percent, could prove to be a disastrous loss of opportunity.

Aside from the United States proper, Europe is among the most important U.S. interests, if for no other reason than the large number of American military assets committed there. A treaty reducing the conventional forces of NATO and the Warsaw Pact in Europe (CFE-I) was signed in Paris on November 19, 1990. That treaty, however, as the first in an intended series of treaties, left significant aspects of European conventional force reductions undecided. Regrettably, the gulf crisis has overshadowed the entire follow-on treaty process. It has also obscured a significant attempt to circumvent the first CFE treaty. Instead of destroying conventional weapons (including tanks, armored cars, and artillery pieces) in accordance with the treaty provisions, the Soviet military has simply moved them east of the Ural mountains beyond the geographic boundaries of the treaty.[4] The controversy surrounding that development threatens delay or cancellation of the February START summit. As in the case of START, American interests are best served by locking in the remaining aspects of a conventional forces treaty while the political situation in Europe, and especially in the Soviet Union, remains favorable.

The proliferation of weapons of mass destruction is an important long-term security interest because of the direct threat those weapons pose to the United States. The collapse of the rigid bipolar security system, under which nonsuperpower states were either allies or clients of the United States or the USSR, means that the superpowers have lost a significant degree of control over the military behavior of smaller states. The effect of that development is to increase the threat that weapons of mass destruction will be used by states that no longer feel, or indeed can be, restrained. In particular, many developing countries in addition to Iraq are interested in chemical or biological weapons as an alternative to expensive and difficult-to-acquire nuclear weapons technology. Some of those countries are also developing ballistic missile capabilities. Eventually, the United States could be endangered. An additional problem in this regard is that the 1972 ABM treaty, designed to balance U.S. and Soviet strategic capabilities, forbids the deployment of a strategic missile defense.[5]

Given those developments, immediate attention should be paid to proliferation issues. For example, it would be prudent to explore with the Soviet Union the possibility of renegotiating the ABM treaty to permit both parties, each at risk from smaller states or terrorist attacks, to deploy ground-based missile defenses. The present concern of the United States with Iraq's nuclear and chemical warfare capabilities underscores the need to develop and advance policies to deal with proliferation rather than simply react to developments elsewhere.

Conclusion

In early November a Pentagon official was quoted as saying that one-eighth of regular U.S. uniformed personnel, or 40 percent of U.S. combat troops, had been deployed to the gulf. He further stated that supporting personnel participating in Operation Desert Shield would include about 70 percent of our total military support personnel, and if an additional 200,000 troops and three carrier battle groups were deployed, the percentage would rise to 90.[6] The percentage of U.S. military personnel dedicated to the gulf crisis is an egregious misallocation of resources and illustrative of the all-consuming nature of the commitment President Bush has undertaken.

The president has concentrated the bulk of his attention and that of his administration on the gulf crisis from its inception. Such an obsession is dangerous because other developments far more critical to long-term U.S. security, such as the internal upheavals in the Soviet Union and Eastern Europe and the proliferation of ballistic missile technology, are not waiting on a resolution to the gulf crisis. They are still evolving, but they are obscured by the preoccupation with the gulf crisis. Other developments, such as the movement toward a European security system and the removal of trade barriers, are being short shrifted by the obsession with the gulf. The window of opportunity, for both encouraging positive developments and avoiding negative consequences, is of finite duration. The disproportionality of the administration's perspective is contrary to long-term American security interests and needlessly endangers the United States. We must not allow our vital security interests to be hijacked by the administration's preoccupation with the gulf.

Notes

[1]For a discussion of a hierarchy of American security interests, see Ted Galen Carpenter and Rosemary Fiscarelli, "Defending America in the 1990s" in *America's Peace Dividend* (Washington: Cato Institute, 1990), pp. 12–13.

[2]William Dullforce, "War Could Suspend GATT Talks Indefinitely," *Financial Times*, January 15, 1991, p. 18.

[3]See *Arms Control Reporter*, 1990, p. 407.B.310.

[4]See Quentin Peel, "Gorbachev Put to the Test by an Army Flexing Its Muscles," *Financial Times*, January 9, 1991, p. 5; Quentin Peel, "Moscow Report Tells How Thousands of Tanks Avoided CFE Count," *Financial Times*, January 10, 1991, p. 4;

and Lionel Barber, "Washington Tries to Read through the Vilnius Smoke," *Financial Times*, January 15, 1991, p. 6.

[5]The terms of the original treaty allowed two exceptions: each signatory was permitted to deploy an ABM defense around its capital and one ICBM launch site. The 1974 protocol reduced the number to one site each. Although the Soviets have retained and upgraded their system in Moscow, the United States dismantled its remaining system in 1976.

[6]*Aerospace Daily*, November 13, 1990, p. 265.

About the Contributors

Doug Bandow is a senior fellow at the Cato Institute, a nationally syndicated columnist, and a former special assistant to President Reagan. His articles have appeared in numerous journals and newspapers including *Foreign Policy*, *National Review*, the *New York Times*, the *Wall Street Journal*, and the *Washington Post*. He is also a frequent guest on major news shows. Bandow is the author of *The Politics of Plunder* and *Human Resources and Defense Manpower* and is currently writing *Defending America in a Changing World: The Case of Korea*. He received his B.S. in economics from Florida State University and his J.D. from Stanford University.

Michael E. Canes is vice president of the American Petroleum Institute, where he formerly served as director of policy analysis. He has also been an economist at the Center for Naval Analyses. His articles have appeared in the *Middle East Review*, the *Journal of Energy and Development*, the *Journal of Business*, the *American Economic Review*, *Applied Economics*, and the *Oil and Gas Tax Quarterly*. Canes holds B.A. and M.B.A. degrees from the University of Chicago, an M.S. from the London School of Economics, and a Ph.D. in economics from the University of California at Los Angeles.

Rosemary Fiscarelli is a foreign policy analyst at the Cato Institute. She is a specialist in foreign and defense policy whose work has appeared in the *New York Times* and *USA Today Magazine*. Fiscarelli is also the author of "NATO in the 1990s: Burden Shedding Replaces Burden Sharing," Cato Institute Foreign Policy Briefing no. 1, and the coauthor of *America's Peace Dividend: Income Tax Reductions from the New Strategic Realities*, a Cato Institute White Paper. She received a B.A. with distinction in international studies and French from the Ohio State University and an M.A. in war studies from King's College, London.

Leon T. Hadar is the former United Nations bureau chief for the *Jerusalem Post*. Previously a fellow at several research organizations, he is now writing a book on U.S. policy in the Middle East and teaching at the American University. Hadar's articles have appeared widely in such publications as the *Journal of Defense and Diplomacy*, the *New York Times*, the *Washington Post*, the *Columbia Journalism Review*, *Middle East Insight*, and the *World & I*. His undergraduate degree is from the Hebrew University in Jerusalem, and he is a graduate of the Schools of Journalism and International Affairs and the Middle East Institute at Columbia University.

David R. Henderson, formerly senior economist for energy on President Reagan's Council of Economic Advisers, is an associate professor of economics at the Naval Post-Graduate School and an editor for *Fortune* magazine. His articles on oil and energy policy have appeared in publications such as the *Wall Street Journal*, the *Energy Journal*, and *Regulation* magazine. Henderson is frequently interviewed on radio and television.

Robert E. Hunter is vice president of regional programs and director of European studies at the Center for Strategic and International Studies. He served on President Carter's National Security Council and was its director of Middle East affairs from 1977 until 1979. He was also a member of the U.S. negotiating team during the West Bank–Gaza talks and the principal author of the Carter Doctrine for the Persian Gulf. In August 1990 he was an adviser to the congressional leadership during its visit to the gulf. Hunter is the author of many publications on the Middle East, Europe, and the Soviet Union. His B.A. is from Wesleyan University, and his Ph.D. is from the London School of Economics.

Gene R. La Rocque is director of the Center for Defense Information and a retired rear admiral of the U.S. Navy. During his 31 years of naval service, he commanded numerous warships and served for seven years in strategic planning for the Joint Chiefs of Staff and the Chief of Naval Operations. A recipient of the Legion of Merit, he also taught at the Naval War College and was the director of the Inter-American Defense College. The admiral frequently writes for the op-ed pages of major U.S. newspapers and makes guest appearances as a military analyst on television programs. He is the host of the weekly television program, "America's Defense Monitor."

Christopher Layne is a senior fellow in foreign policy studies at the Cato Institute. He has written for *Foreign Policy* and *National Interest* and is a frequent contributor to the *Los Angeles Times*, the *Wall Street Journal*, the *Chicago Tribune*, and the *New Republic*. Formerly an associate of a Los Angeles law firm, Layne holds a J.D. from the University of Southern California Law Center, an LL.M. in international law from the University of Virginia Law School, a diploma in historical studies from the University of Cambridge, and a Ph.D. in political science from the University of California at Berkeley.

Charles William Maynes is the editor of *Foreign Policy*. He served as a State Department foreign service officer specializing in arms control and disarmament issues and as a congressional aide before joining the Carnegie Endowment for International Peace, where he has served as the institution's secretary and director of its international organizations program. He was President Carter's assistant secretary of state for international organization affairs and was responsible for U.S. policy in the United Nations. Maynes graduated magna cum laude from Harvard College; was awarded a Rhodes scholarship; and earned First Class Honors reading politics, philosophy, and economics at Oxford University.

William A. Niskanen, chairman of the Cato Institute and editor of *Regulation* magazine, was a member of President Reagan's Council of Economic Advisers. Formerly the assistant director of the Office of Management and Budget and director of economics at the Ford Motor Company, he also has served as a defense analyst for the Pentagon, the RAND Corporation, and the Institute for Defense Analyses. Niskanen is the author of *Bureaucracy and Representative Government* and *Reaganomics: An Insider's Account of the Policies and the People* and coeditor of *Dollars, Deficits, and Trade*. He holds an A.B. from Harvard College and M.A. and Ph.D. degrees from the University of Chicago.

Sheldon L. Richman is senior editor at the Cato Institute. A former associate editor of *Inquiry* magazine, Richman has written on foreign policy and the Middle East for the Cato Institute, the *Washington Report on Middle East Affairs*, *American-Arab Affairs*, and *Liberty* magazine. His articles have also appeared in publications such as the *American Scholar*, the *Wall Street Journal*, the *Journal of Economic Development*, the *World & I*, and *Reason* magazine. He is a graduate of Temple University.

Peter Riddell has been the U.S. editor and Washington bureau chief of the *Financial Times* since 1989. Formerly he was a financial reporter, a property correspondent, an economics correspondent, and political editor of the *Financial Times*. Riddell is the author of *The Thatcher Government* and *The Thatcher Decade*; a contributor to the *London Spectator*, the *Listener*, and the *New Statesman*; and a former radio and television broadcaster in Britain. He was a regular presenter of "The Week in Westminster" radio program. Riddell read history and economics at Dulwich College and Sidney Sussex College, Cambridge.

Gerald F. Seib is currently the White House correspondent for the *Wall Street Journal*. In the early 1980s he covered the Pentagon and the State Department for the *Journal* before being transferred to Cairo to cover the Middle East. He has received several journalism awards, including the 1990 Gerald R. Ford Foundation prize for distinguished reporting on the presidency. Seib received a journalism degree from the University of Kansas.

Richard K. Thomas has been the chief economic correspondent for *Newsweek* since 1970 and has written and contributed to dozens of cover stories on economic developments in the United States and abroad. A former financial editor at the *New York Post*, Thomas has received numerous journalism awards, including two Loeb awards. He has been a guest analyst on C-SPAN, CNN, PBS's "Washington Week in Review," and other talk shows. He graduated from the University of Michigan with a B.A. in English and studied at the University of Frankfurt am Main in Germany.

About the Editor

Ted Galen Carpenter is director of foreign policy studies at the Cato Institute. His work has appeared in numerous journals and newspapers including *Politique Internationale,* the *New York Times,* the *Washington Post,* the *Wall Street Journal, Harper's,* the *Los Angeles Times,* the *Chicago Tribune, Reason,* and the *National Interest.* He is the editor of *Collective Defense or Strategic Independence? Alternative Strategies for the Future* and *NATO at 40: Confronting a Changing World.* A frequent guest on radio and television programs, Carpenter received his B.A. and M.A. from the University of Wisconsin at Milwaukee and his Ph.D. from the University of Texas.

Cato Institute

Founded in 1977, the Cato Institute is a public policy research foundation dedicated to broadening the parameters of policy debate to allow consideration of more options that are consistent with the traditional American principles of limited government, individual liberty, and peace. To that end, the Institute strives to achieve greater involvement of the intelligent, concerned lay public in questions of policy and the proper role of government.

The Institute is named for *Cato's Letters*, libertarian pamphlets that were widely read in the American Colonies in the early 18th century and played a major role in laying the philosophical foundation for the American Revolution.

Despite the achievement of the nation's Founders, today virtually no aspect of life is free from government encroachment. A pervasive intolerance for individual rights is shown by government's arbitrary intrusions into private economic transactions and its disregard for civil liberties.

To counter that trend the Cato Institute undertakes an extensive publications program that addresses the complete spectrum of policy issues. Books, monographs, and shorter studies are commissioned to examine the federal budget, Social Security, regulation, military spending, international trade, and myriad other issues. Major policy conferences are held throughout the year, from which papers are published thrice yearly in the *Cato Journal*.

In order to maintain its independence, the Cato Institute accepts no government funding. Contributions are received from foundations, corporations, and individuals, and other revenue is generated from the sale of publications. The Institute is a nonprofit, tax-exempt, educational foundation under Section 501(c)3 of the Internal Revenue Code.

CATO INSTITUTE
224 Second St., S.E.
Washington, D.C. 20003